# LOST OASIS

I0500230

Copyright © 2002 Douglas W. Hiser, Jr.
This is a work of fiction and any resemblance between characters in this book and real
persons is coincidental.

All rights reserved.
This publication may not be reproduced, transmitted, in any form or by any means,
electronic, mechanical, photocopying, recording, or otherwise, without prior
permission from the publisher.

Cover art by Doug Hiser

ISBN 1-58898-752-3

# LOST OASIS

Doug Hiser

greatunpublished.com
Title No.752
2002

# LOST OASIS

# Contents

"IN THE STALL" 1995 LAGNIAPPE and 1996 SHARDS OF LIES

"WINTER'S GIFT" 1994 BAWL READINGS

"SNOW VISON" 1992 Voices of America

"SHARDS OF LIES" 1993 Winter Book and narrated on *The Voice of Poetry*-Editor's Choice Award 1996 SHARDS OF LIES

"THE JET'S ROAR" 1993 First place award Houston Poetry slam/Catal Hyuk

"THE TRIBE, ASKEW, THE SEASON OF THE BLOOD, OUT WEST, THE SEVEN RAGES and NIGHT IN THE DESERT" 1996 Poetry Portfolio 1997 SEVEN RAGES LUST TO LOVE

"PURR OF THE PANTHER" 1997 Oasis Readings

"PIG" 2001Zero.com poetry 2001 WHISKEY MOON

"ASBESTOS" 2001BAWL CONFERENCE 2001 WHISKEY MOON

"DRIVING SLOW" 2002 Painted Perfectly Poetry.com 1999 TAACCL publication

"ROAD RUNNER BILL" Best Poetry Bay Area Writer's Conference 1998

"WHITE FLAG" 2000 Chinese White Flag Dolphin Conservation Society

Many of these poems and excursions were written between 1991 and 2002. My life and writing has evolved and changed throughout the years so I have included many different types and moods of poetry because I wanted to reflect a complete artistic document of my evolution as a poet and a writer. Poetry is the purest form of the intimate awareness of an author. To read a poet's words is to learn about the author through glimpses into his realm of imagination and emotion. This collection of poetry is a compilation of emotions and observations that affected my life and my world.

# INTRODUCTION

*I began writing poetry as far back as 1978. At first it was just* thoughts and feelings about my life or the world around me. Maybe that is how many poets start writing but at that time I had never even really read any poetry. My poems from those early days were serious to me but only because they held my emotions not any real writing skill. Not all of my poetry is successful, but about one in every ten, I feel like, stands out as something powerful and unique.

I grew up in Santa Fe, Texas in the seventies and lived a life of chasing wildlife and staying outdoors as much as possible. I think catching snakes with my bare hands in the ponds of Galveston County gave me a reckless courage and a vitality of life with a healthy respect for nature. I am a member of Bat Conservation International and an avid conservationist. The world around me constantly is being raped and destroyed to make way for housing editions and other concrete establishments and the animals have no where to go. They are dying every day. I hope some of my poetry helps in this fight against the destruction of forest and habitat. My poem, "White Flag," describes the plight of the Chinese White Flag dolphin.

I have competed in a number of poetry competitions and many poetry slams, where poets read and perform in front of literary audiences. Many of the poems in this collection are more compelling when read out loud, while others have to be internalized to touch those hidden emotions. "The Jet's Roar" is one of the most frequently read out loud poems that I have ever written. It is also one of the earliest poems in this collection. As with a great deal of my poetry the subject matter deals with sexuality, nature and pop culture.

This collection especially illustrates the natural world in metaphor and analogy with a colorful and exotic use of animal and natural description to bring to life the emotions and the stories in the works. A large percentage of my poems do not rhyme and the poems that tend to rhyme are usually just accidentally filled with an inner cadence.

My absolute favorite performance poem is "PIG." The poem is ten times more effective when performed. My wife, Gayln Hiser, has inspired many poems herself and I produced a chapbook known as Treasured Embrace dedicated to her. Many of those poems are contained in this book.

Music has influenced my poetry in a number of ways. Peter Gabriel, Pink Floyd, Al Stewart, Madonna, Rick Wakeman, Fluke, Genesis, are but a few musicians that create a mood that stirs my writing. Poet's writings that have inspired me include, Anne Sexton, John Gorman, Alan Ginsberg, and Mark Sanders.

I have written other books that include, BITE OF THE MAILMAN, SECRET GROTTO, CAVERN OF THE EGGSTONE, DEAD SNAPPING TURTLES, SHARDS OF LIES, THE SEVEN RAGES, WHISKEY MOON, TREASURED EMBRACE, and ELUSIVE REALM. This collection is titled Lost Oasis because I had planned it as being a companion piece to Secret Grotto. The art on both covers depicts a world where fish swim in the air and each contains surreal places and situations.

I am also an artist and owner of Art-Escape.com

Dedicated to my wife, Gayln Hiser, and to Darla Sharp, my friend, who listened and encouraged my writing in the early days.

*Dedicated to my wife, Gayln Hiser, and to Darla Sharp, my friend, who listened and encouraged my writing in the early days.*

# ROAD RUNNER BILL

The sound of a wasp trapped between two panes of glass.
Dripping water.
Moans that you make, sighs of air, throaty gasps as you writhe.
We are materialized in a comic book romance of sex and sin.

I can run as fast as Roadrunner Bill, skating across the ground
after only one hour of sleep in two days, walking like a karate
kid in a black and white movie from Hong Kong, drinking Coca
Cola to stay awake and energized the way those brain cells are
bouncing off racquetball walls, multi-faceted octagon rooms
within the parameters set up by her and her friends.

Terrible gulps of her scent, my face wanting to disappear
between her thighs.
I can feel tears forming and then flowing.
Then they are falling upon her beautiful eyes.
She is meeting me in spaces between the lines, I end up reading
the bookmarker instead of the book, I revolve around her
expectations like a dead caterpillar stuck to the bark.

There are more wasps between the glass.
Multiplying buzzing insects, poison wicked stingers dripping
like water, exuding intense pain, dizzy, spinning, terrifying lust,
anaerobic palpitations, breathing thick clods of gathered dust
through clenched teeth, spiders crawling between cavities, rope
burns on my neck, pantyhose stuffed into my mouth, smeared
lipstick all over the walls, hundreds of wasps gathering forces
between the glass.
The buzzing intensifies like droning ominous bass or the deep
pops of the fires of Hell.

But I am Roadrunner Bill, fastest quick kill on blurred feet,
dodging electric tumbleweed, leaping licking flames, tossing
out the shards of the Art of Noise to take in Prodigy.

I am innocent in my dreams, a naked baby giggling in a room full of sexy bikini nurses, a weird séance calling back her strange name, princess, queen, acid lover, tattoo goddess, turtle belly, heat seeker, kisses that cut like a thin heated razor blade into my soul.

Dripping water.
She is in heat.
I am.
Sizzle.
The wasps are inside my skull.
Thousands of searing stingers feeling like her wild kisses.
I am hers.
I am random and unparalleled, receptive and iconoclastic, alone with the wasps.
I am drugged and free, imprisoned and shaken, clutching and breathing of her scent.

She is desire.
She is sky burning flames, nuclear fusion, electron smashing, microwave-able.
She is the sound of herds of wasps, flocks of wasps, pods of wasps, schools of wasps, prides of wasps, hives of wasps, nests of wasps, millions, zillions of wasps attacking the inside of my mind, my brain, my love and emotion, my cranium lit up with infinite stings.

I am listening to the dripping water.
Listening to the constant buzz.
I am Roadrunner Bill, lying in a dark room with wasps in my head.
And there is not a single coherent answer to anything I have felt yet.
I am Roadrunner Bill and I just keep running like hell.
Into more wasps as far as I can tell.

# THE BRINK

Slippery moving with you.
A rhythm of slow lunges, soft bites,
sliding down your backbone.
My tongue like a snail, leaving a wet trail.

Bucking in the wetness.
Searing flesh, our eyes, locking fast.
Sending jolts into your soul, love, desire,
fill you like electric fire.

And we touch the tips of our tongues.
And our eyes drink.
Travel together to the brink.

Swallowing passion, consuming you.
A nuptial dance of swirling flickers, soft touches, sweet desire.
Sliding down your abdomen, wet navel, my tongue like a nail,
piercing your heart, leaving a trail.

My wet eyes blink,
fighting those tears,
we travel again to the brink...

# GOD'S PINK CADILLAC

Riding in God's Pink Cadillac with Angel's wings on the hood.
Wearing my pajamas, wind tearing at my eyes, and then I
remember that I forgot to brush my teeth.

The striped toothpaste...
And I like the striped gum and we all love the striped horses,
the last animal in the dictionary.

There are no traffic lights in the clouds.
No roads in Heaven and my best friend said, "You're on a roll,
Boy! Go, go!" But I remembered that it never rolls uphill and
I was sad again.

I can be beat harder with words than with my Dad's belt.

Riding shotgun in God's Pink Cadillac,
cruising the clouds in my pajamas,
driving around watching what's happening down on the
ground.
Too bad I'm no longer around.

All the people always told me to watch out,
that I was different, had different rules.
But I know the truth, we all are the same.
Same DNA, in our jeans, same worries.
That's when the spaceships came and changed me.
They took me to a place called Egypt.
Talking to me in thousands of languages,
I couldn't pick up a damn word.
I was shouting at them too loud to be heard.

I'm shouting right now.
At my Mother.
My Brother.

My Sister.
My Father.
My few friends.
Too loud to be heard.
 Naked.
An alien heart.
They changed me and charged me, and made me different.
And I like it.
Except for the tears.
And I can be beat harder with words.
I am damaged but not broken.
And I like it.

God never lets me drive,
because he knew what I did when I was alive.
My shouts echo loudest now,
in my children's hearts.

The spaceships pass God's Pink Cadillac in the fast lane.
How did I ever stay sane?
My alien heart made me different, but I like it.
Except for the tears.

# NIGHT IN THE DESERT

Dry gritty dirt particles press against my skin, lying face up, eyes closed, palms open, fingers splayed out like albino tarantula legs, waiting.

Oxygen intake hot breathing slowly swelling rib cage, dying sun, sneaks away, cactus shadows stretching like tall buildings in a power outage.

I can still see those crooked sentences as they emerge from your open mouth forming elusive veiled words that hang in the air, tangible for only seconds as they evaporate.

Behind my lids colors melt and shift and swirl.
Naked skin peeled back by cool breezes.
The pain, thousands of cacti spines dotting my body, long forgotten, remembering the words you spoke, the stance, the bite, alienation, alternate ramification, lying in the dirt like a pulsing doppelganger.

The blackness pushes down heavy moist thick oozing like ruin blotting dead petroleum and my eyes flicker open.
The sun is gone.
The wind shifts gears.
Crawlings about in the dirt, far off grunts and squeaks, surrounded by ever increasing, escalating sounds, all around, dried blood chills my skin.
My body is like a fallen cactus, spines covering each pore bleeding open.
In the chorus of horror I can hear the words you spoke above all the desert's din.

Somewhere I think God watches from a hidden cave.
White beard upon a wise primordial ape.
He can see my yearning for Coca-Cola.
He is aware of my fantasy of two Asian women.

He blinks at my thoughts of salvation.
He understands the depths of my love.
He lets me suffer.

The sun rises.
I open the ice chest and drink a Coke.

# LITTLE SHINY STONE

I am the little shiny stone at the bottom of the pond.
Always looking up at the surface of the water,
watching the ripples from falling leaves and leaping fish.

The ripples began as little rings, silver and green and white.
Little ever growing circles of disturbed liquid.
Tiny growing waves going to all of the pond's edges.

I am the little shiny stone beneath the shimmering surface.
The ripples never come back to the center.
Lapping at the shore they disappear.

It is very dark and green in these depths.
Heavy tree limbs slick with algae abound.
Tadpoles wiggle erratically over me.
Waterbugs dart like carnivorous predators.
Lily pad root systems hang down like man-o-war tentacles.
Minnows play near the surface, shiners dart like lightning.
A large red crawfish moves his antennae and flexes sharp
crooked claws.
An oval shadow moves across the mud, snapping turtle glides
through the murk.

I am only a little shiny stone at the bottom of the pond.
Tears are not noticed underwater.
The water is purple at night, bright green under the sun.
The tadpoles leave the water one day to leap onto the shore.
Little stones stay in the depths, thrown there by indiscriminate
hands.

# SCATTER BEE EYES

I am calling like a circumspect bull moose, bull whale, bull mongoose, bull shit.
Smiling like an explicit jack-o-lantern, jack of diamonds, jack that went up the hill with jill and jenny, meg and penny, jack of desperation.
I am sitting in a crooked chair, dialing touch-tone redial like a straitjacket tie-die monkey.

My hair is short and grows the wrong way.
I am lying on cold painted floors amidst music CDs, open and closed books of origin theory, extinction philosophy, reproduction cycles of leaf-nosed bats, classic X-men, art history neo-classical text,
exploration of the surrealists.
I am lying in an inextricable jumble
of my own supercilious creativity.
My unfocused nature lies in complete, infinite, disarray.

I am the puzzle, not life.
I am missing a few of the pieces.
I can't find any of the corners, any of the right angles,
to finish the whole picture.
Searching in the residue of real life, footsteps retraced to the primordial beginning to find there is no end to a galaxy of visual images haunting tempting blurring all edges.

The wolf of time chases my heels
like some untiring super constitution.
Howling at dark times, down times, licking his lips as he nips with sharp saliva dripping fangs
at the space between my shoulder blades.
I am sending.
I am calling.
I am patiently waiting to be revealed...

the consecrated curtains of my soul to part.
My iridescent core pulsing in every emotional opportunity.
Dek tobble enoi.
Dek enoi finis.
Scatter bee eyes locking with mine.

I am the paradox.
I am the contradiction.
I am the mystique.
I swim in the cabalistic dominions.
I am calling from the Y and the Z, to solve for X.
In a desert of desolation I am comida.
In an ocean of glowing plankton I am an armada of satisfaction.
In the cold of atmospheric mountains I am, condensed in a can, nuclear heat.
In my own mind I am the Rubick's cube, the mind twister, the repetition of infinity, the source of hurricanes, creation, spontaneous combustion, the question of how all life is centered on the pleasures of sexuality.

This esoteric written is eternity calling.
I am roped to this chair, outside, in the center of the dust devil.
I am sucked dry by she-arachnid, the denting of her cheeks, vacuum slippery.
I am filled with just one kiss.
I am half-empty-half-full crucified on a satellite dish on the Great Wall of China.

I am sprawled-my own blood dripping from my forehead... my nourishment.
There are flashes of landscapes of flesh, multitudes of pretty eyes, parted lips, whispers and gasps, intellectual dreamscapes, exposed film, open legs inviting snapshots, private stolen glances, glimmer parties, Que rojo ohos, bleeding for me, splatter of juices all over the mirrors, gleaming lipstick on my

pillow, intoxica fragrance wafting on the currents,
Dek tobble enoi. Dek enoi finis.
I am filled with just one kiss.
The scatter bee eyes locked with mine.

The casket will close.
There will be tears.
On a table will be an unfinished jigsaw—scattered pieces
without corners.
All my words will pile up and burst into flame.
My children's children will be reading fragments of observation
in the flying black ashes.
Maybe they will be able to find the corners.

# HOOTERSVILLE

Take your dream,
Take it past,
Take it to the last dragon.
I must find a safe home for my dream.
Away from the nervous war...
Jonny Quest and all the rest found your pyramid.
Mighty Mouse and the alien cats fought that war,
Alongside Aaron the alligator.

Battle dredge, Braveheart urge,
Kiss the toes of the Lady Godiva,
And take your dream to the Snow Queen.

Robin Hood told the story...
Spock the Vulcan, Thor and Asgaard,
And the savage sword of Conan,
Flash Gordon disliked Ming,
Elric of Melnibone and C3PO on the back lot,
Gathering dust and magic in the dream.

I saw pretty, lovely, beautiful, mysterious Daphne
Sitting on floating lily pads in warm September
By the bronze giant statue of Apollo.
I saw her secret dream...
Filled with the saddest tears and tallest trees...
And far away jungles where Tarzan stalked, Ka-Zar walked,
Sheena talked to Zebras and Flamingoes while the people of
Pellucidar lived hidden from the sun,
At the Earth's core, in a prehistoric war.

Don't succumb to their killing dreams,
Chase the fireflies while catching dreams in jars...
Ah, take your dream of love and life,
Immortal and X-Man,

Amazon and Jackalgod,
Illuminati and Arachian,
All waiting for you there,
In the dream of Neverwhere.

In the cool shade of an incessantly talking tree
I flow exquisitely free, singing inside, teased by the luscious pull,
The dream of the ultimate dare.
Follow me there.

Lucky Ducky, Cocky Locky, the little scary spider sat beside her,
Cockle burr, Buddha's belly and the rabbit's foot,
And one more thing I saw through the branches,
The sky was blue like a lost lover's eyes
And it shimmered white-blue like a gramma's hair.

With eyes in the back of my head I see,
Syringe slipping in between vertebrae,
My temples pounding with sharp, spiral screws...
Twisting , turning, tantalizing the dream cells
And I whisper out loud where only ants and amoeba can hear,
"Anybody with this dream, take it to the last dragon,
take it past, make this dream last, the fire, Godzilla's atomic blast,
Gigantor's iconoclast, Ultra-man's silver mask, take your dream...
And follow like Mary's lamb turned into a ram."

The NFL and the AFL fought this war.
RKO and KING KONG,
Judy Jetson Porno star,
Diaper man drunk at the Cheers bar,
Banana Splits and Kitterick on a swing,
Chuck Berry Ding-A-Ling,
Clouds in her coffee, Rat Fink on a pencil,

You and I watching our dreams go past
And the ravings of a madman...
... Catcalls from the stage-
Behind the stage, where you and I kiss
Draped in purple curtains and deep shadows...
And we dream of vampires of lust and life...
Me kissing my wife.

Take this dream and shuffle it in the cards,
Tarot cards, call me now, royal flush,
Sit next to me and hush sweet charlotte,
And spin your web...
Talking pigs, flying nuns, cannonball runs,
Three girls swimming naked in the water tower.
I dream of x-ray eyes, big "S" on my chest,
Hanging upside down like Batman,
And when I'm through with stories and games,
I'll walk that dream path of art and comics,
And each day I will realize my life was never the same...
As other folks.
So my dream takes me here and there
I follow it still,

And I will retire in HOOTERSVILLE.

I have fought the war,
Saw a dragon in my life,
Married my loving wife...
Chased a dream...
And led a life of charm and sadness,
Smiling with serious abandon,
I've seen whales and the Astrodome.
My dream has finally found a home.
I end up in HOOTERSVILLE,
They don't have spicy wings
But they have many mundane things.

# THE CURSE OF CREATIVITY

The splintered summer night casts eerie shadows as my despondent psyche delves the indeterminate realms beyond the candlelight and the ambiguity.
The tortuous path of illimitable creativity bears the sharp slashes of razor edges and the slowly penetrating cold steel of the saber.
It is early night and my soul yearns for stability.

Rarely do I wish for normalcy, the gift, like a hidden addiction is too attractive.
The pain of possession,
The endless search for reasoning,
The shift of the soul is like the pulling of the tide.

She is my sanity and my savior.
She is my compass and my comrade.

I reach out from the lonely pool,
Across a distance but only a dream away,
And grasp with the depths of my love,
A single strand of her hair,
In the restless fingers reserved for my art.

I follow my unique capacity to infinite places.
I discover, each time wonderful arenas the world would never find without me.
I am led by the special phenomenon that lives within me,
Led to uncover, locate, originate, and conceive these areas of special perception.
In the darkness I dream desperate insecurities plague my mind
But in the light of her I bask...
Vigorous and vital like a rocky pinnacle watching over a cold ocean.

I once forgot my blessing and pushed the images of the origins from my soul.

For years I sought ordinary and mundane existence, soothing maintenance,

To calm my anxiety and trepidation of surreal and lurid barrages of inspiration...

The life was cold and untrue, following false paths into the undemanding future.

She came to me in August.

Celestial support and the security of the bond of blood,

She is the source of hunger and initiative,

My motivation and my desire,

She is the soaring wing over the rocky cliffs that I stand upon,

Looking down at life's impaling jagged boulders,

Timeless and steadfast like her blue eyes.

# IN THE STALL

The scent of pine reminds me of naked, lazy kisses, shadows, mirrors, of shivers.
I sit in the middle stall listening to the empty tile brushed clean by electric toothbrushes.
Smell pine as I watch pinecones roll on the ground like, oh, like legless baby armadillos, searching... my eyes...in the stall.

Sometimes I am a bull: Smashing, snorting, bellowing, kicking clouds of thick brown dirt, and rolling my brown eyes wildly, remembering her.
The scars of the ring through my nostrils remind me of the frustrating electric pulse,
the splintered pain inside, the bright razor dragged slowly across my cocked throat,
and the devastation of the smoking barrel going into the depths of my ear.

The scent of pine reminds me of safe woods and clean coffee tables,
of rolls and rolls of soft two-ply, of a puddle of heavy clothes around my ankles, a rusty chain keeping me isolated in the stall.
I can see my distorted face in the chrome of the door latch.
I see the way she looked at me when she told me those lies that I longed for.
Those lies I sucked in, vacuumed up,
swept the sound of her voice inside to keep me alive...
To keep me alive in hell.

# THE TRIBE

The water moved like a snake dying.
I stood next to the tallest tree in the middle of the desert.
Gazing far out in the winds of sand.
Mirages masking maniacal visage of the tribe.

Merging with the bark, sinking slowly into the tree, metamorphasizing botanical plane of original existence, molecules interlocking ancient codes of life.

Water shimmering, washing my feet, my roots like a flowing fleece.
I stood inside, a part of the tallest tree, surrounded by sand and snow and wind and tears.
Gazing far out across the desolation.
Seeing the dream of what was once a tropical forested planet.
Millions of life-forms.
Millions of people.
Millions of cities.
Millions of trees.
Cut down.

# GUM ON MY SHOE

Gum on my shoe.
Can't take another step.
Tricks on the brain,
cards won't interpret.
Trouble is my face,
and lucky are my moves.
Gum on my shoe.

Sitting alone in a cantina dream of beer and blue,
I wrap around my table and stool.
Sucking in the second hand smoke like perfume,
I cry a little more and memories fill the room.

*CHINESE Acrobats, juggling life and love*
*painted faces like Mardi Gras masks*
*glow in the dark lips and lost silk panties*
*and black finger nails a haha secret lust.*
*CHINESE Acrobats in the cantina*
*drinking alone of beer and blue.*
*Dancing by myself to a lonesome tune.*
*Gum on my shoe.*

And I forgot the way home yesterday.
And I remember I used to have a friend.
And then...the beer whispers in my ear,
"Have another sip, another song, stay until the end."
Trouble is my face and my words are nervous edge
and I lost my razor and my comb.
Wish I could just crawl back into the womb.
This night is always the same night
of beer and blue and second hand smoke, too.
Gum on my shoe.

My ex-wife is another man's pride and joy.

My other ex-wife is just a ploy.
The other ex just stays on the phone
and I sit here sipping beer all alone.
THE LAST HICKI I HAD...I GAVE MYSELF'
TWO PINCHING FINGERS,
HURT LIKE HELL BUT AT LEAST IT FELT.

I forgot the way home last night
or was it the last night but the bottle was here
and so are my tears.
And I forgot where I work
when I did...I did,
but they spit on me
and beat me so many times
it made me start writing these stupid little rhymes.

*I feel silly with gum on my shoe.*

# BECKONING OF THE ANANIAS

In the hierarchy of those who speak
she continues down a righteous path.
Shadows fill the road before her like tar pools.
She glides across the sticky on gilded words.
Untruth began at birth,
the pain of expulsion from the womb,
and this one didn't cry.

Her place of falsehood sequestered,
in halls of Pyrite, rings of Zirconia adorn her fingers,
and she bathes in distilled water.

The Queen of Deceit reclines on a throne of silk flowers,
clothed in the finest plastic, painted like a China doll,
she beckons me to come closer.
"Trust me."
She says these words with fingers crossed behind her back.

I step forward.
The blade slips in between two vertebrae.
Again.

# THE SEASON OF THE BLOOD

Swimming among the deep dwellers
that have floated to the surface of my dreams...
in the blackest ink of the merging of lost souls,
and the resuscitation of the season of the blood.

*The man stands beside the woman.*
*The woman holds his hand.*
*Two profiles, one looking forward, one looking backward...*
*visions of resolute oblivion.*
*The man smells the scent of her hair.*
*The woman feels his strength of skin and sinew.*
*Two beings at this one place,*
*this moment, this fragment of time...*
*The lost souls touching in the resuscitation of the season of the blood.*

The angles of the pyramid shift.
The deep dwellers swim in the blackest ink.
Flying comets cast fleeting shadows...
over the twisting landscapes.
My hair rises like a whirling tempest.
I rise up from sweaty slumber, eyes open in the dark.

*I lie next to a woman.*
*The woman drapes a delicate arm across my skin.*
*I cannot blink away the visions of resolute oblivion.*
*I smell the scent of her aura.*
*She breathes in my exhalations.*
*The shadows cover the room like black monsters rising up to charge*
*upon the woman and the man in their helpless entwining...*
*Monsters waiting for the resuscitation of the season of the blood.*

And in the surface of my dreams
the angles of the pyramid shift,
blood oozes slowly down the slanted walls,

a threaded needle passes through my eyelids,
sewing shut stitches,
red tears filling up between the sewn lashes.
And in the surface of my dreams
the pyramid spins in a tornado...bizarre whirlwinds splash the
atmosphere with terrible lightning flashes, electrical bursts of
power arc chaotically in the sky behind my eyelids.
Red and purple beams of intense light fire up the darkness in
geometrical patterns, huge dagger-like teeth open and close
with a strobing effect as the goliath roars and maniacal screams
of terror fill the space I swim in.

*Sewing shut stitches.*
*The woman breathes peacefully.*
*She sleeps in tranquility...*
*Unaware of the resuscitation,*
*Unaware of the season of the blood...*
*Sewing shut stitches, silent screams signifying solitude.*

# Driving Slow

Cowboy hat pulled low over my eyes,
I drive my truck into the thick Texas night.
I stare at the white stripes on the highway
And my thoughts turn to you.

I imagine you are right beside me in my truck.
I can feel your warm touch on my arm.
I can smell your sweet fragrance next to me.
It would be so easy just to cry right now.
The air is too thick and the night is too dark,
Without you.
I am driving slower than I have to.

I love the spirit of Santa Fe, southern Texas small towns,
Fresh hay, tall grasses, tallow trees, crawfish castles and
The way your hair blows in the wind like a horse's mane.
And I love holding hands with you in the pasture of my youth.

I am driving slow and feeling the residue of a friend's funeral.
Tears still have shadowed memories upon my cheeks.
I could hear the echoes of the angel's words reverberate around
me.
I am blinking back the moisture.
I am thinking of you and of love.
The world is lonely sometimes.

I saw a lone snowy egret today out in the marsh.
As still as a mimosa tree,
As solitary as me in this truck on this dark highway,
And I dwell on how I stand alone, patient like the egret,
Waiting, searching the water for the continuation of life.

I yearn to fly into sunsets.
I dream of sleeping in on Sunday,

My heart next to yours,
And my life curled up beside me.

Cowboy hat pulled down low.
I hide the moisture on my cheeks.
I drive slower than I have to.
I feel as if you are sitting next to me,
And I search the dark highway for your eyes,
Watching me.

The air is too thick and the night is too dark.
And my soul searches for you.
I can hear you whisper to me on the wind.
Words that slip into my heart like ghosts.
Home is getting closer and the wind dries my face.

I keep driving slower and wish you were here.
My cowboy hat slips lower and I glimpse a flicker of lightning.
I can't hear the thunder only your whisper in my ear.
A whisper of forever love.

# TSUNAMI

This is the contemplative arena within my displaced heart.
I traverse methodically like a desert traveler, a wanderer...

This is the infinite sequestered landscape,
There is sand as far as vision allows
 In all bombastic directions.
This is my explicit personal desert.

I arrive at despondent glimmers of delicious waterholes,
That dot the barren landscapes like surreal promises,
Surreal melancholy hallucinations of the promise.
The promise of quenching my delirious thirst.

I slake my intense craving only temporarily.
My deepest desires lie dormant like a massive tsunami.
I can feel my heart's tsunami restlessly slumbering.
I feel extremely too much,
Reach introspectively inside myself too often...
Watch the memories of lost loves
And dreams I wanted to come true...
Like old home movies in my video brain,
And the tears flow like clear,
Pure springs from a secret source underneath it all.

I search the infinite sequestered landscape
Upon stumbling emotions,
Disparaging tribulations, sorrow flowing within my veins like
My lifeblood, leaking out of my tear ducts late at night
As I drive lonely freeways....
Heading home, heading home...
To an empty house.
A barren landscape, sheltering an emotional sweetness Beneath
the surface.
I await release of the tsunami,

Dreaming on the couch,
Sleeping with the television on all night,
Like a voice of a soulmate.

The desert calls my footsteps to continue.
I quest onward in search of the expanse of water,
Sipping at waterholes along the way.
She is out there, hope is the carrot in front of the tsunami.
She is the never-ending water. She is the overflowing lake. She
is the unknown.
I put these words on paper to heal myself.
She is the answer. She is the solution.
Solve for X...she is X. X=the lake.
I will drink for a lifetime from her...
Never stopping at waterholes again.

My displaced heart, a sanctuary for the sleeping tsunami.
Longing to hear the voice of my soulmate,
I long to swim in her lake,
The water of her, releasing my love, gallons of love,
Passion to cover the desert like a tropical rain forest.
My kisses to the sleeping tsunami...
We would embrace, standing together,
The world is spinning at our feet like an electric globe.
Rain would pelt us like stinging wasps and the drops would
Mingle with our tears of happiness, love and realized hopes,
Dreams that can come true, hearts beating with twin pulsation,
kisses from Eden.

The paradise of the spirit clicking...
Two pieces of a jig saw puzzle.
A merging of X and Y chromosomes
Love, elusive love...
My tsunami.

# THE HONEY TREE

I wrestled with tormented sleep in a tangle of sheets,
my dreamlike thoughts fervidly cascading, changing,
a metamorphosis,
the darkness within me to spectacular rainbows of kaleidoscopic
color.
The honey tree lies deep within the forest.
Its infinitesimal secrets like magnetic forces
tugging me into the prevarication.

I watched her words glide smoothly before me
like ghosts of reality and persuasion.
I could see into her ...visiting briefly with her rapturous spirit.
Walking on this delicate wire
above the perilous pit of wicked spikes,
searching for my eminent sanctuary.,.,.
the place of safe retreat...the place within her heart.

I float in this surreal landscape.
I entwine myself in tangled sheets.
I move like a leopard on the hunt.
I watch the unobservable, listen to the silent,
smell the scentless...

I'm plunging like a plummeting asteroid
towards the softest cloud house in the sky.
Her words are like a map...a guide...a trail of crumbs,
beckoning me to come inside.
Of her.

The clock's second hand has stopped.
The only ticking is my heart.
I am fully aware of the tremendous trepidation within me.
Her vexatious circumstance is questionable.
Her heart is delicate and worth every sacrifice.

And I find myself helpless,
crawling around in my own dreams.

She is my light.
She is the touch at the end of my fingertips.
She is the honey tree.

If I fall I will drag my soul through the pain of sadness.
If I call I will strain to hear her whisper.
If I should grasp her dress with only one finger...
I will grip with such leviathan strength,
such intense passion and love,
such determination,
and I will crawl over glass and lava and endure the hot stings of
thousands of wasps, and feel the excruciating pain of burning
tears covering my cheeks...
just for the chance to be a love in her eyes.
Just for a chance to see the honey tree.
I could die, tasting the honey tree.

I yearn for the honey tree.
Deep in the forest she dwells.
Awaiting my touch.
The sheets are tangled and I cry at night.
In my cloud house in the sky,
I raise binoculars to my eyes.
Scanning the forest,
the dark and inextricably woven nest of trees
and vines and palms and ferns.
I feel the map of her words
and let it guide me into her secrets.

The moon is out.
Black sky.
Listen to the stars gliding about.
The flowers open and close silently.
Bonita.

Amore.
I sit by the window.
The water is calm.
My thoughts are filled with her.
I can see the honey tree.
I could die, tasting the honey tree.

# Whiskey Moon

Amen.
My tongue spits like a cobra.
I lust and wander, creeping and crawling in the night.
I see her as she runs to devour and control,
she is the iconoclastic barbarian of the new century.
She is like whiskey and a tangled infinite forest.
The alligators hide in their dens during the full moon
and the crickets sing quiet songs as the lady of the future
swallows the murky air like a voracious leviathan on a survivor
quest.
I stay out of her way.

Whispers in the current of the bayou tell tall tales of uncanny
creatures
with ludicrous appetites.
Shadows fall across the lawns at the edge of the mysterious
water.
The dark ancient trees sway with crooked fingers bending like
talons
in the midnight breeze.
I walk through the valley of the shadow of the full moon.
I fear no evil.

Junior and his night heron friends stand still like Egyptian
jackal statues,
Poised for darting sharp beaks at unsuspecting wriggling
crustaceans.
I creep and I slink and I prowl and I slither.
I hide in the obscurity of my humanity in the time of the
magic.
The seven runes arranged on the shrine of the jade panther.
I hear an owl sobbing.

The new age of awareness merges with the enlightened souls
like a candle flame flickers in a catacomb.
When she strides forth in a visual form, the insects go silent.


I see her by the shrine of immortal earth
and the two thousand souls enflamed each year are like tiny
fervent cocoons
awaiting her touch of searing passion and thrilling mastery.
The mighty trees bend slowly backward as if a tornado had
wrought their spines
and uprooted their reverence,
and the owl flies away like a ghost demon afraid of the devil.
She is translucent and perpetual.
And as I watch from solitary concealment I see flowers began
to push up through the earth like the skeletal warriors from the
Hydra's dragon teeth.
Her feet are swarming with twisting and turning flowers
dancing about the soil, bathed in an aura of supernatural
origins,
maybe from Heaven, maybe from Hell.
Maybe I should cover my eyes and flee this place of power and
mystery,
flee this time of lunar sortilege.


The moonlit orgy of sensual ecstasy portrayed by ghostlike
nudists, flows,
Oozing like dripping honey from a bee tree.
I am aroused, as hard as the trees, as secret as the shrew,
enveloped by the flames of craving.
She is covered in twisting flowers, penetrating a
nd spilling pollen in orgasmic episodes of flesh and flora.
The moon stares down and saturates its stare with the mist of
an alcoholic vision.
She is a drug, she is a nymph, she is jungle and darkness,
she is the first taste of whiskey...
And the gut burn.

Amen.
So I creep and crawl away in the night.
Aroused and unquenched like a blue knight with a blunt sword and skittish steed.

# THE WOODS EDGE

At the edge of the scary woods I stand,
Like slow water or rumbling clouds
And the depths whisper...
With haunting, invisible, mysterious terror.

The crackling of twigs and sticks snap, snap, snapping.
The wind afraid to disturb the eerie serenity
And my blood is thick and slow
Like that instant before the alpha adult calls your name.

I stand there intently peering into the impenetrable chaos of
vegetation.
I stand there about to involuntarily urinate.
I stand there like a piece of ice, slowly melting into a puddle of
trepidation.
And I here my name called from within the trees.

A calling as chilling as a broken igloo.
My eyes stare into infinity, open wide,
Wide and bulbous like a strangled screech owl.
Do I dare to step towards the ghostly calling, the cryptic woods,
the certain danger.
Do I dare?

One foot slowly slides backwards as my other slides forward,
Caught between fear and mortal terror, I stand in immobile
indecision.

When I was younger I played on a tin slide.
The height of the slide intimidated us all.
Until we conquered our fear.
We slid each day laughing and screaming,
Flying down the slide with adrenaline and excitement.
Once I fell off the top and ripped my shorts and ripped my
skin...

And poked my eye on a big screw.
Fear came back and my caution returned forever.


I stand near the twisted trees and hear my name whispered like death.
A black shadow moves within the woods.
I almost turn to run.
I almost step forward one more time.
From somewhere far away I hear my dead grandmother calling me home.
And I remember she had a Canada goose with a broken wing.
And I remember she saved me from a large white turkey gobbler with a broom.
I remember she was safety.


In my brain, writhing is a tangled bundle of long sleek black snakes
Like octopus tentacles curling around each other and the terrible hissing...
Hissing like the emptying of the pool float on a rainy Sunday.
I stare at the woods but I see the snakes and the poison and the erect tails of scorpions.


Lightning strikes and in an instant I can see a shrouded form standing in there,
Grotesquely beckoning me with a amorphous hand,
The shadow barely saying my name, my social security number, my birth date,
Licking his lips like a slathering pit bull chained too close to the house.


And then the thunder growls in the distance and I crouch, ready to flee.
The moon dances slowly dodging the black clouds of the approaching storm.
I feel the wind flex itself and a fat raindrop strikes my lips.
I taste the salt of blood in the drop.

I start walking towards the scary woods like a hypnotized
zombie.

I feel alone.
I cry tears as I walk with heavy feet.
I shake and tremble as I feel myself pulled forward.
I try to look back at my house, my love, my life,
I try with eyes frozen like a cracking dried contact lens.
I am alone meeting the scary woods.
Stepping within the tangle of forest I cannot breathe.

As my heart still beats,
My mind calms.
The shadow-man reaches for me.
The trees bend down around me like a cage...
And the lightning strikes nearby in silence.
The sound of the storm is drowned by an overpowering
cessation of sound.

And then I remember our song.
With a wicked cold hand touching my shoulder
And a chill enveloping my skin,
I shake my shoulders free.
I throw snakes and scorpions from my sky.
I embrace the vision of my true love
And hold her like courage.
And I sing our song.
And I listen to my own words.
And I heed them and dance.

Amidst death and fear...
Amidst mystery and uncertainty...
I find the strength to dance.
The hope of the dance sets me free.
The dance leaps in my heart and my soul.
And the trees fall back,
And the shadow flies away in another burst of lightning.

And my home is brightly lit.
My true love calls me home.

I am soaked from cool rain,
A cleansing water from the sky
Pours over my skin.
And my heart beats with renewed passion.
My love is fierce like the lightning.
Our dance fills me.
Afraid of the tin slide,
But in life and death, pleasure and pain,
I will always be dancing with my bride.

# THE JET'S ROAR

Outside the sounds, sounds like jets taking off.
Screaming mechanized roars.
Shake it up, Baby.

And now there is something about the smell of those chemicals.
Erotic chemicals that make me feel, so...good...intense.
Yeah.  Baby, Baby.

Where are the lights?
And the jets keep taking off inside me.
And I am swept.
And I have no legs.
And I can feel and smell.
And I get lost.

There is something sweet moving all over my skin, my body.
Something alive and real and tender and desperate and eager.

Rows of empty desks.
The voice of a woman echoes through the wall.
And I can't help myself, again.
It must be those jets, flying again.

I am covered in feathers and I can smell flowers.
A touch.
A new touch and the screaming jets.
And it is wet.

I used to cry when things didn't go my way.
I used to cover my ears when the jets would roar.
Tears are for special occasions now.
For the moments when I am covered in rose petals and I soar.

With fingers, dexterous fingers, I twirl the soft hair of my ponytail.
Nervous twists. My inner extension. The purple, the jets.
And my time is the night.

I bent down over a waiting river of desire and drank and tried to fill her up like a desert. Sand as far as an all-seeing eye.
And still I could go back and drink and drink.


Ladies and Gentlemen, clowns and magicians.
No, no. A horse is a horse and Mr. Ed can't really talk.
After a trip in the desert I can barely walk.
Mrs. Landers stood in front of the class naked,
and the Beave lusted and so did Whitey and Larry Mundello.
And I thought about her too.
What she looked like without anything covering her young white skin.
I would love to take her in black and white film, delicious sin.

So for these thoughts, thoughts that I must hide under rocks,
lest the goody good people judge me on the outside and cast me out to be eaten by lions and asses and scorned by old ladies with blue hair and fake chompers.
So give me my jets that roar inside me and let me feel the purple,
and let me be covered with feathers and let me loose my legs.
And send me out into the desert.
Again, again, again, until I cannot stand up anymore and I cannot breathe. Until my skin's fire has died down and I am numb.
And the lion's teeth do not pain me.
And those real chains fall away, and I can free my mind.

Passion.
Jets.

Feathers.
And I am swept.
Chemicals...purple.
Don't get the wrong idea, judgment man.
Twisting that little hair.
And I am intelligent, energized.
A sexual battery, on and on.
Let's go to Oz.
A cool place where everyone can wear red shoes.
Make love with Mermaids and Nymphs while sparkly magic dusts swirl all around and we recline on pillows made of golden cloth.

...it is time for a break...and...I unbutton a dress halfway down.
I...I...Oh, there is a whisper in my ear, a calling.
And then beneath the white I left my hurt.
Baby it's my turn.
Those jet engines churn.

For me the Fat Lady never sings, I mean never.
When the lid is closed upon my coffin they better weld it shut.
Really.

For I have been to Oz and know secrets of the sex of the mind of princesses and fairies.
Vampires live forever, but only at night.
I live forever only when my words are read.
Never, ever dead.

There is thunder outside saying my name and then it will rain.
And I can feel her thinking.
And the jets make the thunder seem small.
And the lightning within me could light up all the oceans from their deepest depths.
Wipe those disbelief's from your silly smiles.
Cuz this ain't no lie!

# KILLER OF THE RAINMAKER

I remember Mr. Cosmic Destiny, killer of the last Rainmaker.

Metallic blue skin, wet with slippery liquids.
Clearly I can see his large silver teeth and his confident eyes.
The wind snapping at his cloak, like a shadowed druid.

The last time I saw him, dusk was red-orange and brilliant.
The last Rainmaker in a lifeless heap at his feet.

Mr. Cosmic Destiny stood upon a Texas hill,
like a mutant from my future.
He saw me staring and slowly raised a robotic arm,
his hand closed into a fist, except one crooked finger,
pointing at me.

Like a farmer picks his crop...
Following the cloud's shadow, I would never stop.

Trees shed their leaves each year like eyebrows leave a monk.
I could shed my life, my skin a dried husk.
I could stand upon a Texas hill, swallowing the sky.
I still remember Mr. Cosmic Destiny and how he could fly.

The last Rainmaker's gravesite is gone.
A pile of rocks scattered by coyotes.

Each day I chant the Rainmaker's words,
spilling colors upon white sheets of paper.

And I remember you.
Hiding behind a person, watching...
Watching Mr. Cosmic Destiny point at me.
Or was he pointing at you?

# SHARDS OF LIES

There stood the only one who would pray for pain.
Serious threat of rain and thunder, black skies and terrible lightning.
There stood the only one holding a steel rod to the sky,
begging for the strike.

Smiling with teeth that chew on misery.
Thick like old milk mixing with clotting blood.
Screaming, sinking in the ash and the mud.

I am walking faster and faster, but getting farther away from Heaven.
Shards of lies and the calling of dark skies.
And I can't find my wings in a closet of desire.

There is a small geometrical figure suspended in my brain with hundreds of little odd doorways.

I am afraid.
Outside the storm rages, white fire born in a thundercloud.
Its kiss is loud.
Fear grips me like fists closed upon my life...

The bathtub is filled with brown blood. My eyes itch.
I hold on, tightly.
And I remember kisses from Eden.
Each one like a tiny smooth stone dropped into the black water of a silent hidden pool.

# White Flag

Six-sided room, dark stained walls, flesh crawl.
Chinese actress is singing like siren sonar.
Elevated into a clouded space without wires, without effort,
I swim in smoke.
Color of nothing.
Hong Kong little town of brown-eyes.
I hear a solitary flute woefully mourning the lost habitat of the
river dolphin.

The water is darker today.
The sky is dreary.
The people disenchanted.
I watch for hope to fly from the sky like a mercurial messenger
on a white steed.
They swim in lonely pairs, taking breaths with caution.

In the six-sided room I sit in many corners listening.
Listening to the mourning flute call to them.
Out there in the murkier water they glide like secret ghosts.
I swim with them in my dreams.
Color of nothing.
Chinese river moves along without consciousness.

The air I breathe is their air.
Sleek skin is my flesh.
I gasp for sustenance like the mammalian below the surface.
Propellers twirl with vicious blades hungry for cutting the
smooth skin.
In my dreams I dodge and twist and cry out in the depths.

Lying in the tangled sheets I see their graceful forms swimming
above my bed.
Their sonar fills the room and I toss and turn in this fitful
sleep.

The Great Wall, statues of the Gods, millions of Asia like an
anthill,
And less than two hundred swim in the fresh water of the river.
This will be the color of nothing.
Swimming in the smoke of our memories,
In dark water the transparent dolphins swim no more.

# Texas Pasture

Standing in a Texas pasture with my hands in my pockets, I feel
my own heart beat pound inside of me.
This moment I can feel the breeze in my hair, on my face, watch
the wind touch the tall yellow grass.
I see your face in the sky.

I gave my heart to you and tears cut my face like streams after
the winter rains.
Flocks of egrets fly like silhouetted swans across the vast blue
above me.
I can feel the solid earth beneath my boots, smell the
honeysuckle's fragrance, and hear a lone mockingbird spraying
his copied voices into the silence.
I hear your voice speaking to me of a love, of a dream.

You are inside of me.

I give everything and my soul.
I was taught to love by my parents.
I was raised with cattle in the backyard, pigs in pens, and
roosters as my alarm clock.
I rolled in the smell of thick patches of clover.
I read all the books about life and love.
And I searched for you all those many years.

I lean on an old barb-wire fence post.
There is a hawk soaring above me.
Cattle graze out in the pasture.
I think of our love.
I gave my heart to you and a radiant light filled my soul.
As long as I live I am yours.

Finding you gave me the reason to believe in a magical love.
Finding you, the epitome of my life.

I lean here watching the trees, the clouds, and you are right beyond the sky.
I realize all my dreams are coming true because of you.
I give everything and my soul.

Turning away from pastures, I walk across the dirt and the clover wiping wet cold tears from my face.
I take my cowboy hat off and run my fingers through my hair, letting the wind comb it.
I can see my parents house and I see my mom digging in the flower beds.
My dad works on his trailer in the yard.
I thank God for them.
I thank God for you.
The sun is setting as dusk approaches behind me.

I stop and take a deep breath.
And picture you.
In another world.
The little bats will be flying soon.
Darkness comes quickly in southern Texas.
Our love keeps me alive.
I realize I would give my last breath for your love,
to be held by you, to be kissed by you.
To sleep at night in your arms, your heart.
Never to be apart.

I drive away from the sun towards the moon.
Heading for you.
Towards the rest of my life.
The world can have the sun.
The moon is for true love.

I will always give everything and my soul.
My last breath for your love.
You live in my skies, inside of me.

Circumstance stands between us like an invisible wall.
I drive into the darkness, your face shining by moonlight in the sky.
I tremble with love and ache for you...
for you ...
for you are sleeping...
sleeping away from me.
And our hearts contain the dreams of our true love.
And I give anything and my soul to make them come true.
Because I love you.

I see your face in the sky.

# LITTLE CREATURE

This immobile stance of chilled air and empty spaces
like the ghostly memory of her, fill the room with violet water
pouring in through the southern windows.

I heard a sermon once on a dark clouded Sunday,
Words filled the hollow room like flying shadows above me.
Truth and destiny cannot be denied.
People live out their lives in a higher truth.
Dust and particles we breathe like sustenance.
Love gives us life.

A crescent moon called me outside on a dead calm night.
Crazy desperation.
Trapped like a moth in closed blinds.
Phone ringing.
Ringing with disappointed expectancy,
Futile raging hopes fly across landscapes of wavelengths,
like subtle rainbows dwindling to splashes of vertigo.
Is this the way we will always be...
Is this the way...
Love gives us life.

Isolated nights remind me to say my prayers.
I like to crawl around on the carpet.
I like to bundle up in dozens of thick quilts.
I like to dream of real life.
To dream that it exists somewhere, out there.

Little creature come to me.
I will feed you and stroke your soft fur.
Little creature come to me.
I will keep you warm in quilts.
Little tiny creature with the blue frozen eyes,
Look at me.
Come to me and I will feed you true life.

In this immobile stance I swim in violet waters,
cascading in through my southern windows.
I see her ghost walk slowly across this silent room.
And I swim in the memory of her kisses.
And I dream of real life.

Little creature, come to me.

# Empty Fishtank

I looked down at my feet, broken aquarium glass,
Flopping fat fish gulping deadly oxygen.
The big Siamese smiled, perched on the windowsill, coiled and
ready...
like the woman who broke my heart.

I lost all my faith in a few bloody months, or if you talked to the
CHURCH people,
Lost it overnight to the education devil.
So maybe I should be elected as Bullshit offical, Mayor of
Urine,
School Board Fuckup, the Pope of Hell.
Tell me the solution, yeah, I was raised with pigs and cows.
And I like the smell of hay, and I like my pussy in boots
And we like to fuck in barns with chickens watching.

I looked up at the sky, cracking clouds, dark gray and
ominous...
Like a grotesque frown without eyes.
I looked down at my feet, big chunks of glass slicing my bare
meat.
The cat from Siam, blue eyes shining like an orgy, cracking and
crunching wet bones...
Like the bitch who broke my heart.

*In the darkness, I curled up with the sad music of Yokem,*
*My powerful arms helplessly wrapped around the knobs of my knees,*
*Brought up to my chest. Attempting to make sense. My guts are*
**Leaking out my sides and my fingers can't keep them all in,**
**squishy**
*Intestines spilling out between my knuckles...but there is no blood.*
*This is good...I like feeling this way...in the dark...studying my*
*Broken heart, flopping like a fish, a meal on her supper dish.*

# THE BEEHIVE

into the mouth of fire and spit—torrential ice picks piercing
my skin—JABS LIKE YELLOWJACKET'S LIGHTNING
HIT!

Opening my mouth and tasting the air.
The air from the orange lake, lifting and moving slowly...without,
without...disturbing the giant sleeping snake.

The snake's pit filled with infants weeping wickedness.
Beyond the glow of the orange lake.
Past mutant spawn and BEEHIVES,
*I saw a woman's curving breast, in a turning of her smooth back.*

Hidden eyes,
triple lidded.

My skin, tiny red holes, burns.
Yearns...to be near.
Tumbling through boiling sands of fear.
Fear and the gates of Black Iron.

*Beyond her back,*
*her past,*
*gone.*
A mountain looms.

Gray and purple monolith.
Mountain of silk and lies.
Mountain house of the sleeping snake.
Decorated by a thousand BEEHIVES.

"One more lick of salt, I am complete and then I pause...the
sleeping snake, is coiled and quiet."

She see the lake, the gate, the mountain, the snake.
*She cries in her dark solitude,*
*parked in a car.*
*Her tears shining on her face,*
*like liquid stars.*

He sees the water boiling...frustration.
He sees the gate, locked with iron.
He sees the mountain, monstrous circumstance.
He is aware of the giant sleeping snake.
And he sheds tears upon a Pitcher's mound.
Asking God silly questions,
watching from afar, like a distant star.

Into the mouth of fire and spit.
*He bites her lip.*
She says his name, almost a whisper.
*One more lick of salt, lick of sweat.*
*Thunder and the BEEHIVES drip.*
Wet.

Honey.

# BITE YOU

It is true I still feel like a ferocious animal.
All that I desire is to rend and devour you,
again and again, like delicious meat.
Biting hard upon that soft pink muscle of your tongue.
It's true.
Bite you.

When the stars are watching I feel hungry.
The darker the better.
I can be the scary monster that leaps at your throat,
between your thighs, and chews.
Biting hard on the skin behind your knees.
Hot teeth stings like killer bees.
All over you.
It's true.
Bite you.

I care to tear at the folds of the flower and,
the petals of you.
Rough skin moving like the scary pleasure that will not stop.

All that I know is that you want the beast to eat.
I am hungry again.
So call me like the pure prey that you need to be.
Look into my night eyes and lust for me.
Look  into my eyes and see...
my hunger.
All over you.
Bite you.

I am the animal.
It's true.
Bite you.

# SNOW VISION

Out of the vermilion...havoc.
Cast into the sickening snow vision.

Boiling, boiling, the heat heightens.
Snow vision, like twin beams, static.
Idols of fish and serpents,
sparrows and iron antelopes.

Rising above the boiling, strings of purple.
Singing voices, bells, many different bells.
And the kiss of hazy memories was felt.
Thousands of sweet intoxicating smells.

Plateaus of vermilion.
Sweat beads on an infants brow.
Screams echo, and fainting women fall,
flesh slapping upon the hard, cold stone.
And the Indian stands up, answering the wind's call.

Hardened eyes, weary lines upon a fixed mask.
Searing pain, eerie chants and wooden pipes.
Glancing sideways at the jingling bells.
Cast into the merciless Whiteman's hells.

*And the heads upon the totem grimace.*
*And the heads upon the totem weep.*

Eagles fly, soaring above.
Kings of the sky.
Feathers of respect and honor,
headdress for which they died.

Smoke, dust of thunder.
White bolts dance in a dark heaven.

Massive hooves turning the earth.
Bison herds, bellows, snorting,
the rumbles of death.

Arrows, bullets, explosions of blood.
The bison.
The eagle.

The Indian.
The majestic.
Vermilion.
Clouds.

Snow vision.
Vacant prairies of yellow brown.
Dust devils whirl.
Weeping young Indian girl.

# OUTWEST

Lizard suns on a broken rock.
The doorway is partly open.
Her profile in the shadows.
A cactus wren screams incessantly at the Chaparral bird laughing
back at the quail hopping by a flock of dull brown sparrows.

The man leans against the windmill.
Cowboy hat slung low shading sad eyes.
The water pumps into the trough.
Shadows of the turning blades on the ground,
decorating the lizard like a flickering zebra skin.

One burning green eye peers out.
One strand of yellow hair curls in the breeze.
One curve of a small breast.
And the doorway creaks slowly open.

One finger tilts the hat back.
One creased eye steals a glance.
One curve of a bicep.
And the windmill creaks as it turns.

Lizard scurries beneath a boulder.
Cowboy hat in the dirt.
A cactus wren screams, a Chaparral bird laughs,
a quail hops, and a flock of dull brown sparrows fly away.
And the door is closed.

# AT DUSK

The dusk settles on my shoulder blades like an invisible spirit, weighing less than a damselfly and feeling like smooth porous silk.

I sit near the ocean, bare feet in the wet sand, and watch a solitary laughing gull soar higher and higher in the updrafts.
White wings, gray in the fading light.
I can see his lonely flight as a path I have been thrust down...
emotionally crippled like a lamenting harlequin...
buffeted by a rowdy crowd.

The surf calls my name like the sound of my father in long ago memories.
Wave after wave whispers words of cruel taunts and mocking stings of a man-o-war's intestine-like tentacles.
Moisture forms at the corners of my eyes and salt stings my cheeks.
A drop of liquid rolls down my face.
It must be the humidity.

The dusk settles into my skin and the night swallows the flying gull.
I stand and stretch.
I wipe my eyes.
I pick up a sharp shell and cut furrows into my cheeks.
The blood runs and mingles with tears.
I walk slowly out into the sea.

# Everclear Cage Razor Blade

Narrowed eyes chasing me around that Everclear cage,
That hypnotic haze that numbs even that tiny rage.

They wiggle and thrust that liquid tongue like a smooth
python
Coiling around justified lust, turning to dust.

I an just another number, a wild-eyed buckaroo, that can really
Suck it up, back it up,
A long kiss like an ice coated razor blade.

I feel the fade and take a nap in the big shade.

In the dream I see those yellow eyes staring like hungry cats,
and I
Cannot even breathe, the passion overcoming me,...And they
Pounce and rend and tear and the pain is lovely.
Fiery kisses like a blowtorch of desire,
And the Jester cries, "Hanging on the bull's tail, a purple scent
and a
Vapor trail..."

How does it feel to bite the one who makes you drip,
With a slippery whip?

I feel water,
At the edges of my eyes,
And it tastes like blood.

# THE SECRET OF WARD AND JUNE

It was a quiet night at the Cleaver house
with Wally and the Beaver asleep in their beds.
Ward wasn't home, he was working late.
June was in her bed with the window open,
waiting on her date.

Sheer lace and sexy gloves,
because this night she was in the mood for passionate love.

Eddie Haskell, sneaking away,
slipped out his window, his hair combed nice.
Eddie's feet tippy-toeing like kitchen mice.
June Cleaver waited, all hot with sexy style.
Eddie was a rascal, tricky with his smile.

He ran across the lawn,
noticed Ward's car was gone,
and climbed the trellis with ease,
past the boys room,
and sneaked a peek at June.

June reclined, her hair golden and loose, spread.
Her pretty face aglow,
Eddie popped in reaching low.
A night full of lust.
A teenager with a woman and a firm bust.

Eddie Haskell climbed into her bed that night.
And they coupled in forbidden desire until morning light.
Eddie was late to school and June was no fool,
drunk at a bar and content,
poor old Ward was impotent.

# THE PARAKEET LADY

The scary color of faded purple amidst foolish old women.
Talking about killing redfish with dynamite.
Amen.

They keep their teeth in Kerr jars like pickled figs.
Talk about the peeling back of turtle shells.
Soup for the family.
The family of swollen bones and wrinkles.

Faded purple gown draped on a dusty chair.
Forever, since I was a kid, that white and blue hair.
Living on a screen-in, A porch.
Singing low with her parakeet.
Old women talk about Saturday night Bingo.

She's been shrinking and her eyes are fading.
Purple.
Pastel.
Dashing bolts of lightning.
Amen.

Flopping fish, all the curly fingers, slipping.
Leather lady scaring all the little children.
Haunted porch of the Parakeet lady.
PURPLE GOWN.
Moving like a ghost on the dark porch.

The trees in that yard.  Scary.
Teeth in a jar.
Soup for the family.
Amen.

# The REAL SANE

Touch.
Screaming touch.
My room is shadowy and scary and thick and a house of vermin
and images that are alive in other places and they whisper to
me in those moments just before I drift off into a deep RAPID
eye-movement.

Lock...lock my door,
Please.

The pain pulls me into another paradise.
I turn my back and feel wet tongues sliding criss-cross down my
vertebrae.
My eyelashes are glued shut and six Q-tips protrude from each
ear canal.
I don't want to escape this zone,
this evolutionary plane.

THIS IS THE REAL SANE!

I am in my room. Alone. Clouds and moving voids caress.
Curtains flap and I bite my knuckles and taste the syrup and
taste the blood and feel nothing and everything. I can see
hundreds of wicked flashing demon eyes and Angels flicking
feathers of fire and I knew that I was dead and that I could
never die and I knew more than the reasons why. And Holy
Moly to those who sit in judgment and damn those righteous
sweethearts and kiss my ass and kiss my face and put my hand
into your liquid. I don't care if you get it or not. Sweep the
floor. Remember to pick up your brains as you hit the door.

THIS IS THE REAL SANE.
MY EVOLUTIONARY PLANE!

Unlock the door as you leave.
This is a delicate story I continue to weave.
As you go look one last time into my eyes...
You will know me.  You will want to return.

Touch.
Touch as I drift off the edge of the sleepless world and into the
whispers of the real sane.
That one guy who walked on water, I want to know how deep
it was.

# INTO THE OIL

Opening doors to find other doors, without windows or light, under the tunnels of a sister's sight.
I wish I might go on forever just kissing sticky honey and feeling the swarm's stings.

This trek of patterns, ever unfolding, across wastelands of smitten wanderers, trudging through desolation and pent up desire, falling to their knees in the desert's fire.

A man with an iron forehead and blinking yellow lights for eyes stood tall upon a lonely dune, his eyes blinded by white glare of past loves and his prehensile arms folded like tentacles around his heaving chest full of despair and sorrow.
He looked to the sky and began wishing that he was alive.

I watched him tremble, a statue of living flesh, and felt hot tears on my face and a heart that wept like a lost starfish falling out of the sea, beyond our dreams of love and hate, Father's praise and Mother's ways, and all the children without a voice casting oyster shells into the oil.

I open another door to find another door, without caring...
THE ANTS MARCH ON, THE ANTS MARCH ON.
EATING FLESH FROM BONE, EATING FLESH FROM BONE, DREAMS OF A SAFE HOME...DREAMS OF A SAFE HOME. DREAMS...

And the swarms of hornets and the swarms of bees sting my mouth and my lips as I taste their delicious honey.
As I taste.

*A cloud came down to circle me, vulture of vapor.*
*Waiting for the falling, the dying in the sand, the hand...*
*too weak to turn another latch, to open, another door.*

Ancient bark in the door of wrinkled hide, holding honey for the nectar tribe.  Old tree standing without legs or feet upon eternity and I smell the sweetness of what lies within the cork, the dark.  And fluttering wings of cellophane make glittering rainbows of sunlight as they fly into the tree and out again.

Buzzing insects opening doors and daring my tongue to taste their labor, their love of life...she who would be my wife.

And I started melting in the desert's fire—and I cried out with frustration—and I shouted to the sky—and I called to the Moonbitch to call back her tribe.

THE HORNETS FILLED MY EVERY CAVITY...
THE BEES ATTACKED MY SKIN...
AND I GORGED UPON THE HONEY.
AND THE PAIN, OH GOD, THE STINGING PAIN,
COULD NOT DRIVE ME FROM THE SWEET.
ALL MY LIFE TO EAT.

I am liquid at the roots of an old tree of doors.
A thick brown syrup, without sight, without voice, without life, without flight.
A joining of syrup and honey, and the earth erupted with flowers and vines, patches of soft clover and grasses, and pines, and curly roots, and wheat and seed puffs and cattails and pods.
And another door opened—Dainty feet dared tread, with sparkles and glitter and glowing toes and feathered ankles...did she come...

A cloud came down to circle her.
A cloud of vapor that was me.
Droplets of moisture memories of my tears and wet touches her skin, that faery of mystique-kin.
She glided into the oil, smooth submerging in the black.

The last door opening to the back.

Molecular strands unwinding, little bells jingling with the chiming.

And I was her and she was me.

*A CASCADING OF MERGING MEMORIES OF EVERY LIFE AND DEATH, EVERY TEAR AND LAUGH. AN ELECTRIC JOLT OF WELDED CONSCIOUSNESS AND DREAMS, AND AFTER THE LAST DOOR,*

**WE WALK IN THE CLOUDS BECAUSE THERE IS NO FLOOR...**

# MARY'S KISSES

Mary quite contrary kissed the boys and made them feel like
scorpion stingers punctured their lips.
But she never kissed where it counted, dear boy.
So I swim through the chocolate lake in search of Mary quite
contrary the ghost of all the kisses and the stings.

*The cave is black and silent, I am afraid, I am cold*
*I shiver and shake-rattle and roll*
*love is my drug and she shakes my soul.*

*But the damn cave is black and I am blind as a naked catfish-scared as*
*a jackrabbit with cramps in his jumping legs stranded out in the middle*
*of Interstate Highway 45 at rush hour in Houston, Texas.*

I keep trying to open my eyes wider to see something, anything
but the truth always eludes those who need mercy or sex or
nourishment or chips and dips and wet kisses from Mary the
goddess of all stinging kisses.

And in the chocolate river I gulp And I can see Mary's eyes in
the sky=And the damn cold scary cave is black and part of my
dream that never ends=And my fingernails keep growing and
growing in a circle until they pierce my palm leaving scars like
masturbation or lost love or that gnawing fear of a mid-term
test.

I am in the cave. Mary grins like phosphorescent light.
She is naked to my touch and then the stinging begins.
I have never been the same.

I awaken at night filled with screams,
Mary's kisses stinging in my dreams.

# THE ARENA

Into the arena
silky stockings
sleek-supple
lust
want
fire
exotic-woman-feminine-sex-fantasy

Burning in the arena
flesh thoughts
undressing
caressing
naked dreams
erotic-girl-nude-pouting-desire

Dying in the arena
watching her move
envisioning skin
passion and kisses
in my mind
alone-at-the-bar

# ROCK TOSSING BY THE WATER

I always dreamed I would be the only one.
Blame has never flown in a straight line.
Besides you and I,
there were clouds,
of rumbling thunder and wicked flashes of lightning,
the pain in our hearts.

I have always chased partial rainbows.
Sadness swirls like a lost hive.
I sleep in a shadow mist.
And then there are the clouds above my bed,
of thunder and pain,
of the lost love that I have missed.

Slow my pulse in the presence of a waking dream.
Those eyes burning into my hidden desires.
I walk sometimes by the water,
re-assembling decisions,
second guessing the reasons why,
and leaving my mistakes in the depths
by tossing a round rock in with a splash.

There are still no answers.
My questions are supposed to drown with the rock.

# POLE

Suspended from a splintered pole.
Ribs exposed with dried blood.
Sent out in the world with colors.
Bleeding for the Geometric Priestess.
Reader's Document. 1993.  Covert concubine.
Lightning dash.
Eerie flow of incoherent transmission.
I can see upside down.
From the pole.
In the wastelands.

Bleached bones.
Ashes on the ground.
Picked clean.
Vulture-Buzzard-Carrion-Flapping shapes.
On the pole.

Eye-sockets.
Black holes.
Inverted.
On the pole.

Like a nude dancer,
clinging and spinning.
The straight, solid pole.
Phallic.
Death.
Covert concubine.
Geometric Priestess.
Reader's Document.
1993.

# THE FRUIT OF EDEN

I stand on one leg,
leaning against a dark wall.
Thoughts erasing other events of no consequence,
relative to any justified outcome or elusive ramification.

The winter wind moves strands of my hair across my forehead.
Streetlights seem like metallic giraffes with only one eye.
The pavement is cold and hard and shadowed.
A cloud of unsympathetic waves reverberates in my mind.
*"If only I could find..."*

I allow myself moments of sweet drifting back.
Sweet visions of isolated pleasure.
Candy and sugar, were those kisses.
The fruit of Eden, smeared all over my body with the juices of
love and lust.
A tear forms at the corner of my left eye,
blurring the forms of the metallic giraffes.

The bottle of beer in my right hand has grown wet with
condensation,
grieving the loss of its contents.
The night has no stars.
The moon is hidden.
I stand on one leg, my other foot propped on a dark solid gritty
gray hard cold empty wall.

My silhouette from one view like a "4."
I throw the bottle.
I turn and run.
The cold wind brushing the fresh flow of tears.
The street is endless.
I cry.
I run.

I want to feel.
I cannot touch.
I cannot escape.
I cannot speak out loud.
The beer is inside me,
like secrets or lost kisses.

*"If only I could find..."*

Falling.
Falling in a ditch.
I curl.
I curl up in ball.
I curl like an embryo.
I am wet and cold and alone.
My eyes cannot stop blinking.

The fear is overpowering.
The regret of the past inaccurate trajectories merging with the marrow of my embodied soul, my ravaged spirit, the inner air of life that extends itself like blood across the receptors, across the living electric points within me, is killing me.

Blood seeps from my tear ducts and I cry in red spurts bubbling on my facial skin.
Cars travel by my violently shaking embryonic body, headlights like vast sweeping terror, as I become something else in the ditch.

I am aware of my heartbeat stopping.
My skin stretches and changes to albino white.
My vision is strobe, infinite blinking.
There is no saliva, no taste, and finally no teeth, no voice.
My ears fold upon themselves and the car's rushing sounds are gone.
I glow in the ditch.
I remember life.

Blood is dried upon my face.
I remember where I have been.
I remember the fruits of Eden.

Turn off the strobe light.
The razor blade falls from shriveled fingers.
Relax.
*"I was not meant to find..."*
Lights out. No need to set the alarm. There is not a wake up call.
Relax.
Relaxation.
I can still smell her skin, damp from a summer rain.
It is all that matters...
Memory of the fruit of Eden.

# ASBESTOS

I am still changing like melting mercury.
I need to dance more often by myself.
I am dead in traffic.
I am hungry for apples.
.
I need to violently smash barriers of negative psychology.
I am living ever after.
I am strolling along with too many cares.

Tonight just kiss me like lightning.
I am melting into puddles of lemon beneath a solitary streetlight.
I only want to chant indecipherable phrases, to hold hands with a penguin, to
play hopscotch with Enya, to sleep in a round bed with snow leopard pelts, to burn with desire,
running naked in the wind, to breathe refrigerator air, to see the future.
I only want to see the future and remember the past like a footprint.

Gargoyles of living stone on the rooftops.
Bizarre images in the living room, flying dark shapes, flapping things.
A broom is lying in the corner, a discarded staff, or a magic wand.

I said, "Love me."

I said, "I am blue. I am here. I am yours. I am in love. I am solid.
I am metallic. I am gentle.
I am asbestos. I am latitude and longitude. I am an umbrella. I am a vehicle.
I am falling. I am stumbling into each daybreak. I am a

caterpillar. I am sheer. I am a proton.

I am drifting like plankton. I am alone in avoidance. I am simmering on a gas flame.

I am eve's dropping on God.


When God said, "Get on with it!" Adam kissed Eve and all her sisters and the planet was populated. There were crying babies everywhere. Adam was in the Garden drinking beer with the snake and coming home drunk to all
his wives making more babies.

So I can hear the "Get on with it." in my head without the babies crying.

And I sleep in peaceful wet arms attaching themselves to my skin like the slippery suction cups of Octopus
tentacles.

.

I can feel the dance in my veins.

I can sense the trance traveling up my vertebrae, bone by bone.

The dance courses in me.

I am changing like mercury.

Chemical intertwining on a perverted plane.

I am missing everything.

I want to feel.


There is a Praying Mantis on the window screen.

There is a clock telling time backwards.

Salt flowing upwards to save Dorothy.

She moves in circles, slowly.

I am mercury.

I am liquid, thick and oozing.

I am a cascade of shadows.

I am immersed in the erotic episode.

I am the voyeur.

I believe in this.

Eve ate the apple, the peach, the grape, and slowly ate the banana in front of Adam.

She said, softly, "Move with me. Breathe with me. Get rid of that fig leaf and take me. Get on with it!"

I am the card shark.
I am under the table looking up her dress.
I am living the game of Monopoly.
I am tricky like the "Silly Rabbit."
I am tip toeing across the balance beam between Purgatory and Atlantis.
I am parked at the blinking red lights of the railroad tracks.
I think about her.
Alone in the dark, waiting on a train that never comes.
I am waiting to feel again.
I keep thinking, "Get on with it!"

I am asbestos. I am slipping into the purple. I am dancing with no one on a leopard skin in an empty art
studio. I caress ancient iron weapons.
My fingers can do anything.
Rocks are my friends.
Trees make me nervous. They can get angry and throw fruit.
I am fireproof. I am changing like mercury.
I am the last star that disappears at dawn. I am living a
dream. I have opened my eyes only a few times in my life.
I am dead in traffic.
I am in this strange hot vibrating paradise of Heaven and Hell,
saying prayers to the zillion minds
of God.
I chant to disperse the antagonistic strangling stress.
I shift and change to mercury, to asbestos, to the chant, "Flame
on, flame on, flame on."
I am there.
I am in thousands of windows in her mind.
I am mercury and asbestos and the Praying Mantis.
I am the voyeur.
It feels like nothing else.
I am apart of it.

Everyday, tears form at the corners of my eyes,
Sometimes without a reason.
I am dead in traffic.
Inside of me there are no borders.
There are no paragraphs.
Inside of me there are no right angles.
There are no answers to traffic.
It feels like nothing else.
I am apart of it.
I am swimming in the lake of tears....
Eating apples with the snake.

# ANSWERS

The answers are found in little piles.
There is only personal right or wrongs.
Slow down for me.
Take the pace way down low.

Anger and conflict are scars that cover me.

Shuffling through the depleted deck,
as I get older,
stacking aces when I can.
Trying to cheat myself to win.

Moving too fast for me.
Slo-motion for me.
Take it slower.

No one needs to understand.
No one needs to feel into me.
No one needs to test me, change me,
war with me, kiss me the wrong way.

I will try to crawl all the way home.
Past the arguments and the smoke.

This is how I write when I am drunk..
Where is that little pile of answers?

# PIG

Into the dust.
I want a glimpse of the scatter bee's eyes.
Tricky walking the wires.
Into the crust.
I want to touch the silky hair of a fortune cookie.
tricky, wishy, lucky, crushing with clipped fingernails...painted black.

I am decorated with question marks.
Styrofoam contact lenses.
Drinking honey in sticky gulps, licking like a bear's tongue.
I want a test of abstract answers to jigsaw seance ouija quiz-a-thons.

Into the moving spaces around the floating bodies at the mall.
You are the one that isn't there.
Humming silent whispery lyrics that scroll down in front of my face like an iridescent adding machine, a spitting printer disposing of x-fodder, a wheelchair for plastic dolls with winking eyes, and the sky is filling with the swarm.

Big teeth inside a pig's ear.
And we once locked fingers and spun the secret combination.
Now I cannot remember the numbers...LEFT-RIGHT-LEFT.

Pigs should love.
Pigs should lap it up.
Pigs should dance naked.
Pigs should touch themselves.
Pigs should float.
Pigs should swallow.
Pigs, pigs, pigs, wallow like leviathan sex objects in cooking oil and peanut butter.

Into the dust.
Into the crust.
Into the silky hair of a fortune cookie.

Broken watches adorn my expectations.

Question marks like big barbed fish hooks digging in my cranium.
Make my body spasm, jerk like a shocked mudpuppy on serious acid.
Jump little pig.
Wah La...see the pigs listening like a line of wanton pinup girls. Pigs in Alta Loma. Pigs in Canada. In Russia. In Monday thru Friday. Pigs in transition. Pigs in bikinis, skirts, jeans, astronaut's suits with big snout bubbles. Pigs flying by with bat wings. Pink pigs wearing panty hose. Pigs slurping up honey on a newspaper. Pigs on TV, stereo sounding snorts, playing in the beds at the furniture store, calling 900 numbers,
pigs on vacation. Pigs touring the museum, walking through Rome, Paris, Kenya on safari, Thousands of pigs on cruise ships eating and laughing their way to the islands, Bora Bora, Tiki, Bermuda, Galapagos to see their cousins. Wah La...see all the pigs.

My snarling hands clasp my head like a clamp.
I think about vibe.
I am possessed with oriental writing.
I am a slave to the breathing.
I am quick to jump into the honey with the pigs.

Tricky walking the wires.
Nothing is like balancing above a mass of hungry pigs.
Nothing is like tasting the silky soft sweetness of a fortune cookie.
Dancing with scatter bees. Waltzing with cracker sizzle stingers.

Dance fool.

Flesh petals, bloom tips, chrysalis spit, sugar crab, weed fur, fourteen platypus eyes, jumping spider tusks, leather thorn cricket, sad crystal vines, metal dust weevil, ermine tails swishing in the short level cactus hedge, game rutting finchboy.

Dance fool.

Dance with the pigs.

Dance with the scatter bees.

Dance girl.

Dance wild inside, delicate feather face, serene feline of invisibility and sleek midnight motion, caught in the never never act of velvet nature Dance finchboy, dance fool, pig.

Pigee, pigee, pussy pig, pussy pigee, pig, pigpigpigpigpigpigpigp igpigpigpigpigpigpig...

Jump little pig into the silky hair of a fortune cookie.

# X equals Zero

I lie on the floor on my sweaty back, naked like dead prey for flocks of circling vultures.

Inside, my stomach has a hole through which crawls your sickening lust, hate, pain, pleasure, want, desire, fire, your hungry mouth, teeth like sharpened daggers, drooling lips painted with black lipstick.

My wrists are bound with gasoline soaked twisted rags.

My ankles are spread wide, held tightly to the ground with old rusty steel bear traps.

If I could only dare to open my eyes I am sure I would see you standing over me like a wicked emperor, holding a lit match in your clawed white hand.

I can smell the gasoline, my own urine, your perfume, your sex juices dripping in your coming of heat.

"Somethings" are crawling all over my skin, in my hair, into my ears my nostrils, thousands of sticky pointed mandibles testing my flesh.

In my tortured mind I imagine gerbil sized spiders, hamster scorpions, field mice crabs, lobster praying mantis's, bizarre beetles and weird winged insectopoidian arachniphilum creatures playfully marking their edible territory upon my exposed torso.

I cannot comprehend my proud erection standing amidst the terror and the impending pain.

If I would only open my eyes I know you would be smiling a smile like a mannequin or a mime's skull perched atop of my tombstone.

I can hear the shuffling of your spiked boots as you walk slowly around me.

I can hear your grunts of satisfaction, your sighs, the shallow breathing of your heat.

I know you are excited by my helplessness, my evident

desire, my obvious pain, humiliation, embarrassment, shame, perversion, deviance, pleasure, torture, submissiveness, want, fire, desire, succulence, iridescence, burning, scorching, delicious, my persona in turmoil, in your control.

You still hold a burning match.

Yes.

Anything you want.

Eat me. Light me up. Drop the match. Turn me on. Eat, suck, bite, scratch, tear, strip, rip, flip, shred, hit, lick, slip, scrape, slap, chew, spit, grab, turn, head, slurp, grind, knead, caress, pull out my beating heart and set it to the torch.

It is what you want.

It is what I want.

We are crazy to deny each other.

We are always on the outside looking into each other's lives like demented voyeurs.

We are emotional deviants.

We are the number Zero.

We are at the Equator.

We are together. Me in my bondage, you in your control.

I am brilliant. A genius at searching the depths of my feelings. My emotions, the edges of my soul, as close to a pharaoh as a human can be.

And you tear me apart like a scarab beetle eating slowly into me.

We are Zero, We are X.

We are nowhere, in no time, infinite invisibility, licking our wounds with abrasive tongues.

If I open my eyes I know you will drop the match.

But hell, I'm already burning.

# The Owl and the Target

The sounds of some electronic bizarre owl echo across the room.
A mysterious ticking of a loud clock or a hidden Spy vs. Spy black round bomb that looks like a bowling ball with a wick.
And then, and then...

Amazons in bikinis, red sports cars, lace panties, shiny handguns, and palm trees,
and then, and then...
Mitzi Kapture, Rob Estes, and then
I know that I don't have time for a shower until SILK STALKINGS rolls the credits.

I am curled up inside the softest corner of the couch.
At night, the screen my only light, Rob and Mitzi, my friends.
I think about chess moves, old Valentine's, and tic tac toe.
I think about strawberry Popsicles, cling peaches in heavy syrup, and falling out of a relationship like Geronimo.
There is a pair of antlers on my television.
A target for my eyes.
And then, and then...

I go deeper into this reflecting trance.
I fade from the neon of the Palm Beach Police room.
I think about a target for my life.

I'm starving but I don't need much...
I'm not Hungry Jack or Jack Tripper or Cosmo Kramer or even Oliver Douglas, boy he had a dumb blonde for a wife.
I don't even want much...
I'm not Reno Raines or Mitch Baywatch or Inspector Gadget or even Tennessee Tuxedo who at least had a loyal best friend in Chumly the walrus.
I really can't handle much...

I'm not Mannix or Paladin or Rin Tin Tin or even Jethro Bodine
with his really cool bachelor pad.
My goal comes to me clear and it is so simple: Just don't be sad.

The sounds of the owl call to me across the room, whispering to
me in the deepest trance of love and life.
I think about my targets and all those mis-fired darts, stray
arrows, bullets that hit the red dirt instead of the can.
I think too much and talk too much and kiss the right
woman...
not enough.

A target for my eyes.
A target for my lips.
The owl again, SILK STALKINGS, a good mystery, the right
woman,
a best friend, a frenzied lover,
and then, and then...

Curled up on the couch.
Ward and June, Bob and Emily, Rob and Laura, Charlie and
his Angels, Brad and Jennifer, Romeo and Juliet, Robin and
Marion, Mork and Mindy, Al and Peg, Kermit and Miss Piggy,
and on and on,
 the couples walk hand in hand in my mind.
The owl again.
Targets, red and black rings around a bull's eye.
My bull's eye.
Clark and Lois, Tarzan and Jane, Peter and Maryjane, Apollo and
Daphne, Boris and Natasha, Herman and Lily, Bill and Hillary,
Elvis and Pricilla, Fred and Wilma, and then, and then...

I walk through the jungle.
Monkeys in the trees, stone gods watching from the foliage.
The canopy above is filled
with a myriad of bird sights and sounds.

I am naked.

My skin painted vermilion, with violet stripes, deep blue vertical lines, and little dots all over my skin of canary yellow.

Hollow wing bones of fossilized doves protrude from my nostrils and my head is shaven like Mr. Clean.

I walk slowly, with caution, along the jungle trail and some of the yellow bricks are visible through layers of the dirt.

Suddenly the jungle is quiet.

The stone gods close their gritty eyes.

I stop.

I listen.

I am alive.

I hear my own heartbeat, my breathing, and then, and then...

I hear that damn owl again.

The ticking again...and the trail leads to a leviathan target.

A target so immense, so monumental, a target made for Godzilla or the Green Giant.

Bigger than an elephant, a brontosaurus, a blue whale, the astrodome, that space ship in Close Encounters, or the space ship that came out of the ocean in the Abyss.


This target is my goal.

My love.

This target is my life.

I stop.

I listen.

I am excited.

I tremble.


The skin on my back begins to peel like a cool sunburn.

God touches my spine with a shimmering colossal finger
and pushes me forward.

My eyes are wide open sucking in all of the light and I float above the ground like a dangling marionette,
and then, and then...

I am on the couch and I open my sleepy eyes and realize that SILK STALKINGS is over and I missed the ending,

but I heard the owl,
and I saw the target.

I'll just shoot straighter the next time.

# Seahorses

She dwells in a solitary seashell
combing her hair with anxiety.
I can envision her long tail
and her thoughts like twinkling anemone.
When I dream I see through her underwater charade
and I know.  I know, she knows.

We swim through different currents in the same waters like colorful seahorses only touching with the lengths of our long pretty tails.

She watches upward, trying to see what lies beyond the surface, guessing whether it is day or night above the waves.
She watches upward worried about the sky and the air.
I swim crazily about her gulping in our beloved water as she dreams of air.
She dreams of air.
I swim about her knowing it is the water in which she truly cares.
And the sharks take swipes at us with rows of sharp teeth.
And the jellyfish dangle tentacles filled with paralyzing poison.
And the seal lions dart hither and thither snapping mouths at us.
And we swim haphazardly, tossed and buffeted
by the strong currents.
And we somehow cling desperately to one another
just by the lengths of our long pretty tails.
We're swimming, my eyes on her, her eyes upward on the surface.
We swim alone in different directions but always touching.
Always touching with the tips of our long pretty tails entwining together like two secret lovers holding each other with just their little pinky fingers.

# The Scar Cage

This is the destiny.
The wary character of the nether region creeps stealthily in the
shadowed alley
behind my heart popping his knuckles
and licking his wicked lips like a perverse villain
in a pseudo nuclear lamenting nightmare.
Scars on my heart like teeth marks of pleasure and pain.

This is the rhythm.
This is the human condition of despair.
This is nervous synaptic response.
This is the negative child of dismal meanderings.

I came across a soul of smiles.
I bathed in the phosphorescence of the green illumination.
I was inept and beguiled following this false radiance.
I was the lesson to be learned.
I became seduction.
I became the prevarication.
I became the vexation—
crawling through the ashes of despondency in a wasteland
filled with ravaged withered trees,
crooked branches like twisted scars on my heart.

It takes too much energy to recover from this rejection.
It is like i need to plug my veins into a reservoir of potency.
Recharging my emotional status with a flux of positive stimuli,
either that or disappear into the darkest cavern like a recluse.
Emerging months later like an albino with debilitated sight.

A woman's mystique clouds my awareness.
I quest like a lost knight upon a weary steed.
I traverse landscapes of tar pits and deadly quicksand.
Dueling with seven-headed hydras and plagues of blood gnats.

I am driven, fueled by an unquenchable passion.
Pushed by a damaged heart that screams silently for retribution.
My eyes lit like tempestuous beacons reflecting the infinite love within me.

This is me.
This is the life of pursuit.
I am my own prey.
I am carnivorous.
Devouring my own self esteem like a late night snack.

My destination is brilliant and fascinating ..yet ..
so damn obscure.
She is my dream.
She is the unknown.
She is beyond me, out there hidden.
She could appear at any second,
any minute,
any hour,
any day,
any week,
any month,
anytime...please.

I am a cage of scars for enchanted love.

Each scar on my heart...makes me stronger.

# The Laundromat Woman

It was too hot of a day,
Too hot for me.
Slicker-suit JoBob and the Mastodon Cowboy came crashing down,
On my day dream consciousness like a fudge-sicle...
On a melting July Texas skateboarder concrete sidewalk.
 The sun, lunatic sandstorm, rays of ultra-violet masochism,
Sandpaper caress of the Laundromat woman.

I shy away from her lust like a mosquito bouncing on the rolled-up window.
Bluejean Barney and the purple penis intruding on sesame slut street,
As the girls line up for tattoos on their daring does.

Shopping for beanie weenies and poptarts in cowboy boots.
The store is air-conditioned nipple prodding cold.
And there is Slicker-suit JoBob selling pizza samples like a mad clown.
And there is the Mastodon Cowboy singing lonesome tunes,
On an air guitar by the newspaper salesman.
And there is the Laundromat woman,
with Oil of Olay and Coppertone Tanning Butter,
Coming for me,
 on aisle three.

# MY FUNERAL

Black and white checkerboard casket filled with water.
Angelfish swim about my body and my closed eyelashes
brushed their fins.
I hate water in my boots.
This is the perfect picture.

A funeral for me, myself, and I.
Black roses strewn about, as a flower girl marches down the
aisle,
pretty smile painted on like a rodeo clown.
A choir sings with an eerie sound accompanied by a solitary
piano,
a fiddle and bagpipes played by men in skirts, without shirts.
This is my perfect picture.

I am immersed in the casket-tank.
Bubbles follow bubbles from my ears.
This is being dead, so take it to the bank.

There's a photo on the coffin's lid.
A black and white memory of me as a kid.
There's a sword, a bat, and a necklace.
And only a handful present that I could trust.

My palms face up to embrace Angels as they descend.
My self stands like a ghost made of cellophane above the
still living...and I can see a few tears.
I can read a few thoughts.
Most do not understand this creativity, even in death,
that I have wrought.
A funeral for me, myself, and I.
In the final tank, I lie.
This is the last picture to shoot.
I hate water in my boots.

# ALL OF THIS, EACH NIGHT, IN MY CAR

There has been wine and roses a hundred times,
sweet kisses like mercury, only one night I held you-the death-
the poison-the lust-the fear-the love—every single morning and
every single night, I drive alone with my thoughts, memories,
dreams of you.
I feel your breath on the back of my neck.
I sense your eyes watching from over my shoulder.
I can almost feel your fingers trace my spine and crawl playfully
into my hair.
All of this invisible, in my car.

I stare at the highway, eyes locked with yours floating before
me.
I replay your words from last month, last year, eternity's.
I listen to the song, my radio battling the wind from the rolled
down window, and I remember long ago nights,
wine and roses a hundred times.
I feel the wetness on my cheeks, moisture filling my eyes,
blurring my image of you.

It starts to rain.
I try to breathe.
Every night.
You sleep in different arms.

I close my eyes,
rain on my window,
and I feel you touch me,
in my dreams.
I cry in my sleep.

# ASKEW

She reached me, deep inside,
touching places.
Twisting things.
Askew.

In each other's arms,
we were not the same.

She may call to me,
in the lonely twilight.
Turning my heart.
Driving deep.
Penetrating like a spike.
Digging.
Corkscrew.

She knew every emotion,
nothing I could hide.
Long walks.
Gazing eyes.
Matching strides.
Long roads,
that went nowhere.
Fingernails scratching.
Thrusting past defenses.
   Luring me.
         Tugging.
Pulling.
               Chaining.
     Locking.
Eating.
    Biting.
        Freezing.
Burning.

Me up.

                              With Desire.
                  And Pain.

Those eyes.
                  Twisting.
        I can never...
          Never.

                              Be the same.

        ASKEW

# FORTY-FIVE MINUTES...FLYING TIME

Last night I pulled myself out of myself.
Standing over my sleeping person in my bed,
I glided over to the window.
The sky was black and infinite, scary and desolate.
Donning invisible wings I flapped towards Heaven,
quarter past eleven.

Forty-five minutes...
flying time.
Gates of Purgatory...begins the story.

Twelve midnight and I arrived:  Nude Angels in shiny perfect
skin.
A world of naked perfection and without sin.
White wings and beauty beyond the sky,
Heaven's people, all could fly.

Past the Pearly Gates I could see all the Saints,
with faces painted like Geisha's,
high curving eyebrows and chalk white faces.
Saints wearing corsets and panties with pink laces.

I started to cry when I was led into the throne room.
A room filled with a pleasure laden orgy of sex and skin,
but there was no sin.
I cried because I knew I had died.
And I tried to wipe my eyes,
THERE HE WAS...
And I had found out that God was Bi.

# A STAND

There is only black and white.
Gray is a deception and a neutrality.
The lifeline follows a line not an interruption of lines.
The line curves and winds or even circles but it never breaks
until death.

The answer is either yes or no.
You must be on one side or the other.
It is either guilty or not guilty.
You must either win or lose.
The tie is not a result.

The stand.
The middle is crowded with the indecisive.
Take a stand.
Agree or disagree.
Life's short journey doesn't have time for the fence sitters.

Stay on the side of your heart.
Go against your heart and the kisses will feel like pain.

# BLACK ROSES AND CANDLELIGHT

Tonight is our night.
Black roses and candlelight...
The scent of honeysuckle in the garden...
Clouds covering the stars to hide our perverse passions...
Serious obscenities, indecent caressing of alternate skin...

The mist belongs to our embrace.
A lone finch chirps somewhere in the shadowed trees.
The sweetness mingles with our drawn blood.
We bite each other's veins like starved carnivores.

This is our night, tonight, under a black sky.

# A CLUE IN THE SOFT THINGS YOU SAY

I think about your words,
about what you think is wrong or right.
And I tell you how I always think about you
in the middle of the night.

I look for a clue in the soft things you say,
Darling, do you love me always, all the way?
I look at you through my tears, in a park,
I lie awake and see your face in the dark.
And I recall those soft things you say, and I look for a clue...
do you love me always, all the way?

I look into your eyes, across space,
on a lost Saturday night.
I see him sitting next to you and I remember...
you told me you loved me,
and for you he isn't right.
So I look for a clue in the soft things you say.
Darling, do you love me always, all the way?

I can tell when you're with him that your mind's on me,
Darling, love me, set him free,
be in love with me.
Don't be alone on those dark nights,
call to me and I'll be there holding you tight.

So I look for a clue in the soft things you say,
Darling, do you love me always,
even if you choose,
with him...to stay,
love me always, all the way.

# ANGUISH OF THE CRUSTACEAN

The red sky shifts.
I feel closer to your heart.
Closer to the source of the earth deep.
I feel it in this walking sleep.

The scent shifts.
I breathe of you.
Drenched in the pouring of your flesh.

Scenes roll by.
Scenes roll by.
Dreams of the insane.
Melting colors, rainbow pupils, blurred, slurred, violent slashes
of white.
A sea of black and rumbling silence.
Scenes roll by.
Scenes roll by.
Dreams of the walking sleep.

I can feel the mood of the soil.
I can sense the shift of the molten rock, the terrible anguish
of the crustacean, the lost phosphorescent life of the floating
ones.
I can sense your dreams.

And the night comes like a misty rain in the darkest forest.
And the trees stand still and straight and listen as she sings in a
voice like the queen of sadness.
And a single point of light twinkles in the depths of blotting
black, calling back, beckoning to the ever children of the bark,
the souls of the red sky.

Scenes roll by.
Scenes roll by.

Yes...this is inside.
Scenes roll by.
Scenes roll by.
Scenes.

The red sky shifts.
I drift closer to the source of the earth deep.
I feel it in this walking sleep.
And it rains.
Dreams of the insane.

# THE DREAMER'S SEA

Swirling darkness crawls inside of me,
gently touching those ancient memories,
those scrolls of film that hypnotize my mind.

There is a mountain in the near distance,
belching smoke and fire like an angry leviathan
keeping his distance but rumbling in restraint.
This is just how it used to be.
This is how a lost future cannot be made to see.
This is what we sing for.
This is what we drink for.
This is the episode of real life.

In the heart of my darkness,
nudges of fantasy testing the deep waters,
those flickers of strobing images that flash across those endless
screens.

There is a melting sky washing away pain, blasting the core of
surreal islands and driving a hot metal spike into the lungs of
the rock.
There is a standing monolith guarding the gates of convoluted
dreams, confusing visions, plastic, electric, terrifying,
fascinating, magnetic welding of a blowtorch close to the skin,
sealing forever the real.
Caging the rumbling of the restraint.
This is just how it used to be.
This is the dreamer's sea.
This is more than I can see.
And this is what we sing for.
And this is the song.
And this is what we drink for.
And this is the drink.
And this is us and this is suing for real life.

The swirling darkness crawls.
Leap-O. Jump-O.
Flying at your throat-O.
My mind's Jell-O.
She kissed the boys and made them die.
She-O. She kissed the boys and made them die-O.

I sit in my silent silence.
Eyes open.
In the darkness.
There is a sliver of light.
A sliver of sight.
In this sadness.
In this dreamer's sea.

# GRANITE JAGUARS

Jade slate adorning eyes like granite jaguars in a dead dark room.
Seeing through deception of currency and blood.
Decapitation riddles the headless thoughts like absent worry.
Machine bursts sound out alarms to the fires down the street.

Love is bigger than death.

Understanding pure reason delves deeper beneath wet sheets of sweat and juice.
Catastrophe beckons wanton desire and squelches rationalism.
I walk the cement paths of cigarette butts and pigeon droppings,
My eyes focusing on the transparency of my 1.75 contact lenses.
I take short steps to avoid confusion and dodge cracks as wide as baby ribbon snakes.
Daydreaming that I own purple.
Purple, the color.
I own the rights to it.
Every time it is used I get royalty checks.
Purple is popular but white could have made me richer.

White is bigger than death.

Rhinoceros horn appeals to sexual appetites in the orient the way nachos magnetize ache and irregular digestion.
In the bright lights of a wayward priest caught eating girls scout cookies in a country of right and wrong we are mesmerized by hatcheting off at the wrist the afflicting digits.
Dancing with virgins begets worn shoes
and dialing wrong numbers might find you a new psychotic friend.

Granite jaguars watch from the trees above the sidewalk.
Their jade eyes as still as a centerfold.
Coca-cola sipped through a straw with an accordion neck.
The space is silent like embarrassment and I dream again about love.

Love is stronger than life.

At least love continues, like mitosis.

# LOOSE ENDS

Loose ends are open doorways.
Walk into...
Walk out of...
Back in...
Back out...
Loose ends are always open in all directions.
Go in.
Go out.
Nothing is certain.
Loose ends are always untied,
as long as you continue to lie.

# WATER WATCHING

I watch the mysterious water.
never ending ...this flowing body of the sea.
I watch the ripples of minute fish and secret creatures below
the surface.
I watch the setting sun casting her face out on the golden
waves.
never ending...this flowing.

The waves call to me softly in that lost voice.
I smell the skin of memories upon the wind that moves across
the water.
The green, the blue flecks of the sea, the white crests like sad
smiles.
The watching of the mysterious water.
never ending...this flowing.

A tear drops softly into the sea.
A forgotten time of swimming in this emotion.
This endless flowing, never ending.

The ocean is made up of lost teardrops.
The water dominates the earth like sadness in the heart.
A tear drop falls into the ocean while I smile sadly.

The water is darkest at the bottom...
endless flowing...awakening at the surface to the touch of the
sun...
and my eyes filled with tears as I watch your face in the waves.
And I twist a little smile for the sea is never ending...
endless flowing, teardrops falling into the water,
filling up the sea, blending with the waves.

# A TEXAS LOVER'S MOON

The last night I saw you,
there was a Lover's Moon.
The Texas sky was darkest blue
and the air was smooth.

I wish I could have held you,
beneath the Lover's Moon.
I knew you weren't ready,
that for you it was too soon.

On the last night I saw you,
the mystery was all around.
We could have shared the hours,
until daylight we were found.

I wish I could have kissed you,
beneath the Lover's Moon.
I knew our hearts were trembling,
watched by a Texas Lover's Moon.

If I could have that night back,
and we were there again,
under a Texas sky with air so smooth,
I think I would have swept you,
into my arms, so tight.
And beneath the Lover's Moon,
I would kiss you, that night.

And beneath a Lover's Moon,
it should never be too soon.

# LONGER NECKS

I think we need longer necks.
We could see better behind ourselves,
long curving necks like a swan or at least a goose.
We could see under our armpits and between our legs...
for better cleanliness.

If we had longer necks we could...
sit farther away from the table.
We could sit farther away from each other,
and still kiss.
We could walk farther out into deep water.
We would need taller turtle-neck sweaters.

If we had longer necks we could get more hickeys.
We could swallow longer swords.
We could wear many more necklaces.
It would be easier to wash our hair without getting anything
else wet.

We need longer necks to look around corners.
We need longer necks to see higher.
We need longer necks just because they look more elegant.

I think we need longer necks.
Not as long as a giraffe's but maybe a goose.

# PIGEONS

Hundreds of pigeons.
Into the sky.

Thunderous flapping of flight feathers.
Flocks circling.

The statues cringe.

# VISIONS OF RED LIQUID

Tears keep falling down, pouring down like an angry river.
I am standing at the edge of the leviathan.
I keep blinking and winking, closing my eyes to the bloody
downpour draining red liquid, salty and wet upon my cheeks.

I curl up in a fetal ball and consume the wetness.
Tears slide one after the other across slippery skin,
weeping away the sins of the family, the sins of the father, the
sins of the wicked sadness of crying in the bloody night.
Visions of cleansing water obscuring my sight.

He sat over by the bush.
She reclined next to the granite.
Another rested on top of the beaten down grass.
Another, herself surrounded by an aura, floated on the surface
of a shallow, mirrored pool, magically suspended above the
liquid like a flying fauna or nymph of the breeze.

I curl up in a pool of scarlet tears.
Naked wet skin tightly clenching my knees and biting my lips.
I hang on in the outpouring of the blood from my eyes.
Visions of cleansing water obscuring my sight from those lies.
Tears pouring from the sight of those lies.

He left the bush, she left the granite.
The grass stood tall and I felt the shallow water of the mirrored
pool sweeping all around the fetal ball I have become.
Skin absorbing the wetness.
Sponge-like and amphibian immersion I stretch out and climb
to stand.

The pool explodes in a shower of geysers.
My eyes clear.
Diving into the mirrored pool.

Searching the depths of myself.
I find nothing.

# THE SCEPTER

Darkness fills the void of my shaking bones,
when I see you look at me...look at me.
Poisonous kisses injected like vampire rattlesnake fangs
and the sweet smile of rejection crosses that conscious plane,
when I see you look at me...look at me.

My eyes are staring upward in the pool of despair
 thrusting without effort to rise above the murk,
the luscious pain, the scepter of human emotion held by the
naked god of passion
 who watches the struggles of the unrequited.

The sky falls like a roller coaster hurtling through thick blue
oxygen,
when I see you look at me...look at me.
Spikes break through the ground like the enormous spines of
porcupines
and the lovely smirk of satisfaction settles in that awareness of
contradiction,
when I see you look at me...look at me.

My living future screams.
I cannot sleep.
My flesh knots in a warped struggle.
I find myself looking for your eyes in the air.
Into the mirrors and the passing glances into window glass...I
stare...
at your reflection...but you do not look at me....look at me.

*I reach for the scepter..............look at me.*

# SHOOMA KA (WEST WIND)

Runes of ancient oracles are whispered in the old ones circles.
Retelling and living the forgotten rumors of the leviathan and
the smoke
and the chants in the secret cave around flickering firelight and
oil lamps that cast shadows of eerie presences the old ones close
their wrinkled eyelids.
And the howl of the west wind screams as it is pulled chaotically
through the tunnels of the bear and the sabre-tooth.

The gourds rattle as they shake in the steam.
The blood is swallowed.
The horns of the gazelle are lifted high by gnarled hands.
The vertebrae bones are tossed onto the skins.
The whispers begin again.

Shooma Ka.
Shooma Ka.
Bring in the virgin and the snake.
Passing the fruit from elder to elder.
Yellow decaying teeth biting of the fornication fruit.
Shooma Ka.
Shooma Ka.

The fire rises higher.
The bones tell their story.
The leviathan and the smoke.
The pipes make another round, passing within the circle.
The virgin and the snake, writhing.

The silence echoes in the cavern.
Even the west wind curls up in the corner and watches.
The virgin and the snake.
Buffalo head enters, the leviathan phallic man-monster.
The smoke erupts from covered fires.

Shooma Ka.
Shooma Ka.

Buffalo head enters the virgin.
The snake sinking fangs.
Shooma Ka.
Shooma Ka.

The howl of the west wind screams as it is pulled chaotically
through the tunnels of the bear and the sabre-tooth.

# THE DREAM OF SPIDER TEETH

I awaken with an eye full of sand
from a dream of lobster claws and spider teeth.
I sit up in the sweat of my bed
and see horror in the room...
fatalistic images of a cock crowing,
wicked witch on a bicycle or a new broom.

Little blonde girls dancing on pointed toes,
little pink bows on their sheer clothes.
Little ears with odd points in rows,
little desire spreading lust as it flows.
Little yellow-haired, winged nymphets, wind blows,
little fluttering females, around my head, so...

I am asleep again in another land,
the last dominion where things happen again.
Lost in an image, eating cherries and plums,
and I cannot believe I have no body, only a quiet hum.
I can see stars, planets, voids, chasms, a vortex and patterns of
light.
I can see breasts, nipples labia, clitoris, pubic bite.
I am asleep in another zone.
An obsolete place where the only sound is the ringing phone.
Lost in fog and sex, a soul without skin or warm embrace.
Lost in smoke and bitter hex, a thought without fact or even
trace.

I awaken folded in half like a broken revolver.
Bullets for brains.
And now everyone knows that I am insane.

# THE DANCER'S TRUST

Acidic gushing mental hallucinogens
Like impenetrable iron walls of illimitable frustration.
I try to crash headfirst and batter through
But resistance is shadowy and ambiguous.

Guiding me like the rarity of an eclipse.
Swirling me like a dancer in a tornado.
Buffeting me like the lick of fire and the stick of ice.

Love.
Love is purity.
Intimacy cascades with the honey and the wine.
Trust is more elusive,
Like the reflection is opposite in a mirror.
I sleep with nightmare clues of disaster and fear.
I analyze scattered words and protective lies that stay in the
air.
I watch the manipulator play his cards like a professional.

My love endures and loyalty is my honor.
To survive the immoral stalker, the player of lies, the shifting of
reality,
I must delve within and grasp a shaken core.

Understanding is forever.
Duality is uncertain.
A golden ring is only a dream.
Love.
Love is purity.
Geese mate for life.
Goose and gander, never to wander

When will the dancer step out of the winds
To stop the tornado and hold hands with life.

I can see the same water rippling infinitely.
Sipping wine and reclining with a furrow in my brow
Like a mannequin upset with the display window.

# Vague Emotion

The vague absence of cumbrous emotion
Like the staring out the window seeing nothing.
The way eyes see only thoughts.

A river churning slowly,
A sunset staving off the horizon,
Clouds promising empty promises of rain,
A solitary rock enduring eons of erosion,
Like the endless snow of the arctic.

The lemmings follow the leader.
A wave of fur over the cliff,
And the shiver of chilled skin on a hot day,
Brings memory haze into focus.

The way eyes can watch the thoughts,
Like staring into the vague emotion that has no name.

Hypnotic chaos, tangled yes and solid no,
Closing off vocabulary, and the eyes lock in silence,
Impasse of vague emotion,
And that emotion has no name.

Love delves deep.
And blind eyes open inward.
Vision of the heart.

# EMPTY GLASS OF WINE

There is an empty glass of wine on the table next to my bed.
My hair is tangled and my bare legs are hanging out of the sheets.
I miss her already.

This is a lonely bed, sharing pillows with myself.
So I just sprawl like a lazy lion in the dark and watch the digital clock.
And I miss her so soon.

She is gone again,
like the way words are whispered in a dark tunnel.
I cannot even talk to her tonight.
She is a lover with a bite.

Disappearing after spreading magic in the room.
A wild witch without a broom.
Like the Sandman leaving crystals of sleep in my eyes.
Living nights without her is like living lies.
Foolishly sometimes I had wanted to die.

There is a place inside my heart that is like an empty bed.
She is gone again.
I miss her already.
I miss her tonight.
She is a lover with a bite.

There is an empty glass of wine beside my bed.
I hug two pillows tightly and the mane of a lion tangles.
I open my mouth to yawn and sigh.
I fight the urge to cry.
And the lazy lion watches the digital clock.
All night.

# BIRTHDAY THIRTY-SIX

Another day, another year,
My damn birthday is here.
Yippy ki yo, yippy ki yay!
I better get laid.

My sister called and her little girls sang me a song.
Lovely little voices and sweet wishes to me.
I am damn older than I was yesterday, get along, get along.
and now my night is leaving,
and the dream is fleeing,
and the day is going to pass,
and I'll be stuck sitting in front of the TV, on my ass.

Another day, another year.
Happy friggin' birthday Daddy dear.

Dosie do and skip to my loo,
I wish I was still twenty-two.

Thirty-six years ago, I swore with a loud cry,
pulled from a womb...still trying to get back inside another one
ever since.
I think of this night going down the tubes and how it is just as
well,
maybe I'll just curl up and cuss to myself and shake my head...
and feel like another year is dead.

# THE PHENOMENON OF DUST

There is a phenomenon, to live in constantly changing
environments
 and to outgrow each existing phase.

With this statement the teeth grow sharper,
the mouth is open and the daggers show themselves.
To change is to precipitate conflict
and the royal executioner pulls on his gloves and mask...
readies himself for the task.

The ladies cast themselves out the upper windows
and they crash like flowerpots upon the cobblestones.
The king asks why and his jester makes up a lie.
Why does he have to lie?

There is a phenomenon, to adapt to your constantly changing
environment
and to stretch with each existing phase.

With this statement the world speaks louder in a thousand
different languages
and no one ever understands.
Understand the other,
but why do we have to die?

There is this phenomenon, we must change or die.
There is this inevitable phenomenon...it is death.

Death is the birth of dust.

# IT HAPPENS AGAIN

It happens again.
And I say that this isn't real.
And you say that I never talk to you.
And I say that you won't listen.
And you say that it's all lies.
And I say that this isn't real.
It happens again.

# HELLO...HELLO?

There is one friend that I have left,
a friend that I can trust with anonymous bits of knowledge.
Your damn answering machine.

# HALLOWEEN STREET

Darkness, void of stars, absent moon,
trembling child, fearful howling of caged dogs, and the scary
music of the lost wind.
Witches, woman mystique, fascinating whores,
apprehensive housewives behind locked doors.

We walk down Halloween Street listening to footfalls, catcalls,
grunts in the bushes, little squeals of pleasure and pain, eggs
flying through the air, the rustle of paper bags, candy wrappers,
the drip drop of slowly spilled blood on asphalt.

I can see her pale green eyes staring at me.
I can feel their heat singe the edges of reality.
The wine of the night pours over waiting lips,
and the senses escalate, spiraling upward,
above the body, soaring without sanity, merging with the seven
clouds and the eleven deities of the Communities.

We are together, drinking, of our souls,
like a hummingbird's tongue, thrusting into a flower
we thrust into one another, sucking moisture and emotion.
We are together, walking down Halloween Street,
saturated but never satiated.

# NONI'S OLD HOUSE

The old house was full of secret stairways, musty closets, antique trunks with big brass locks, and stacks of dusty papers in the attic.

My Grandmother Noni kept a loud raucous parrot on the back porch and a broken winged Canada goose in the back yard.

I used to sit and swing on the front porch watching the cars go by on Highway 6.

I used to swing and watch the hummingbirds sipping their juices from the flowering vines that adorned the railings.

The old house was full of my Grandmother and her husband, Paw Paw.

They are both gone now.

The old house went down before they did.

Uncles tore rotten boards away bringing out the skeleton of the frame.

The roof shingles were put to the fire after the house went down.

billowing black smoke obscuring the sky and the highway.

Fire trucks arrived expecting to save the old house...
They drove away disappointed as the smoke died down.

The grass is shorter where the old house used to be and sometimes I can see hummingbirds flying by, searching for the flowering vines.

# SUPERNOVA

If knowledge and information are the keys to understanding,
and understanding is like a hard slap in the face...
Wild, sweaty, grinding, panting, grunting,
hot sex outdoors is like being burned in the flaming heat of a
supernova.

# OBSESSIVE LOVE

The sun is larger than the moon.
In the sky they are the same size.

# RENTED WINGS

I can see them carrying me.
Black coffin...black earth.
I can still see her face, those sad lips.
Pink or flesh or rose or...
I can still feel that elusive trust.

I must not watch with closed smile anymore.
She has felt all into me.
Now I can walk in clouds, exist in the surreal.
They have probed all into me.
My wristwatch has stopped.
Even the second hand, frozen.
Perfect.

Everyone is doing those same things. Catching, chasing, running, calling.
I could have had a neon casket.
A strobe-light funeral.
Pallbearers in white tuxedos, like albino penguins.

I should put my thoughts to rest.
Go to a lasting bed, it is best.
Where do we get those pretty wings?
All those flyers above the gates, show me how to do this...how to fly and to float.

Asking old friends, "Check it out."
"Am I still invisible."

Strolling past my old house, mist in my eyes, I was very small.
No one could ever see me clearly, even though I was there, alone, in the hall.
Strange, the way I turned out.
Never a tangible to fall back on.
I should shout.

No, I think I should have stood on a tall hill
and pulled the one that was sought with the strength of my will.
Learning to fly and to float.
That delicate piano played for me that final note.
Smiling eternally, showing my teeth, little sharp teeth.

I always wanted to be all into.  I wanted to fly.
RENTED WINGS.
Strange the way things turn out.

It was not easy for us.
Not much choice down in the soil.
Except for the color of your wings.

Now I am talking one million languages,
and wearing God's white suit and top hat.
Rented wings on the weekend.
Floating, this is where it's at.

# THE SMOOTH

I have been in the SMOOTH...
Cascading soft Angel's feathers, pillowy dark pupils with
infinity oozing...oozing...thickly around my soul.
And I didn't want to come back.

Glancing in mirrors which lead on into other mirrors and again
on into other mirrors, I thought I saw crinkled tiny, sparkling
shiny, elusive iris winding hither and thither and without and
curving around a maze that leads never out.

*and i felt more as i was enveloped by the SMOOTH.*

"I read somewhere about how powerful or was it so powerful?
Yes, it was...AND PURE AND TANGIBLE like the white, yes,
glowing white claws that flash out of the quick, lethal paw.
The beauty of the SMOOTH.
I HAVE BEEN IN AWE."

Touched by the SMOOTH, felt in the SMOOTH, drained in
the SMOOTH, held fast like the tiny amphibian impaled on
barbed-wire by the "Butcher Bird." *But I didn't scream because the
pleasure spread and bled into exotic erotic charges that sped along my
spine, searing my mind.*

*And I am wanting the SMOOTH.*

Long dexterous toes that tremble and grasp and pull out
sensations that were held on thin nerve wires like fishing twine
twisted around a brown milk nipple.
I could feel every motion, every tug, every pull, subtle jerks and
hard tongue slaps, raps about my body like a school of darting
minnows.

Without a word...I can't breathe anyway, I slip, I slowly slide,

I let go easily and drop down, falling in slower than slow motion——a frame by frame advance. A lowering of my mind, my body, my chemicals, and liquids, once again into that endless craving, that SMOOTH.

*Closing my eyes I feel myself becoming black sky...*
*each pin prick of pleasure the million stars..*
*my gasping breath, the atmosphere's winds.*
And I have let go...go...go...gone...***GONE***...nothing but the SMOOTH...the SMOOTH.

ORANGE RUMBLING MUSHROOM CLOUD IS MY SHELL...
and the stars connect brighter light than the fires of hell.
Hungry for enormous gulps of air, when I come back from there.

*my legs are weak...but my heart still beats...*
*and I am groggy and loose...but i want...i want...i want to go,*
*BACK IN THE SMOOTH.*

# VENUS

***In my head I can see the colors of sanity, pain versus ethereal glimpses into my undesirable psyche.

I can smell the scent of 1986, 1993, 1995, 10:00 PM, Friday the 13th. Eating the crust of despair, licking the dried blood of mental wounds, crying to myself, what a pussy I have become in these last few years.

A SLAVE TO LUST AND LOVE AND SADNESS LORDING OVER EACH TWIST OF THE DAY.

Venus, where are you?
The planet is fading out.

In my house there is a statue and another and little monsters that are like me. Talk to me.

The phone has gone, "CLICK." and another voice dies.

Outside in the sky energized golden seahorses glide over my rooftop and I can see faces of chromosomes and the stars are red like the sheen of a cardinal's wing, and God's eyeball peeks out from behind the moon, a big scary orb of awful judgment...and I lie on my rooftop feeling the grain of the shingles on my back. I am naked, vulnerable, because it is the only way to be.

Venus, where are you?
The feminine celestial sphere.

Talk to me.
The sound of digital tones calls in my brain.

Oh, the splitting of searing, sorting, the excruciating anguish of rejection, another blow dealt to my low self esteem, no matter, the stars are not critical, listening without comment, looking at me with compassion and feelings that I can only imagine exist.

Little men with translucent skin, large headed friends thinking, ever thinking, "I don't give a fuck about basketball, baseball, the damn weather report, newspapers, wall fucking street journal, car sales, boats, chainsaws, carpet cleaners, sofas, loveseats, silk ties, fat free food!!!!

Venus, where are you, damn it!
I need to be inside a woman, in the womb, where it is safe and warm.
I need to be safe and making things that no one has ever seen before.
I need to be like a new appliance that needs no batteries.

I need emotion.
Venus, where are you?
Feed me, eat me, merge into the world where we all can only feel.

# BLACK VULTURES

*false smile.*
*riveting rumble beneath textured skin.*
*intelligence chaotic scramble.*
*wipe that face clean.*
*bitch.*

*taste of cold smooth down my throat.*
*thoughtful dilemma.*
*triangled web of deceit, dexterously woven net of luscious lies.*
*tangled strands of indecency, twisted wreckage of my life.*
*bitch.*

I sit quietly on a pier overlooking a lagoon filled with calm water and dotted with dead trees.
Black vultures sit mysteriously on bare branches as white egrets wade in the shallows.
The sun is leaving and the sky is dull orange.
My eyelids blink and I think of vultures and egrets, dark water and dead trees, false smiles and lies, sadness, sadness, like a jar full of collected tears.

I drain the last of cold smooth from the brown bottle,
wipe my face with the back of my hand,
stand on tired legs and sigh, breathing out to blend with the breeze.
I watch one vulture flap lazily out of a tree and into the darkening sky.
I watch the black shape disappear at the horizon
and I turn to go, looking back at the water one last time, wishing, wishing...the lies were real.   *bitch.*

# FROM YELLOW TO ORANGE

I'm thirty-eight
learning that I'm not a kid anymore.
I'm sad more often than not.
It's just the way the sun sets, from yellow to orange.
But this is the way it will be
no one is the grown-up for me to lean on,
for me to call for help, for me to cry for.

There isn't any going back.
I'm the grown-up that sobs...easier each day and in the dark of
night,
and in the solitude of driving around.
This is the new me that I have found.

Everything used to be so, so yellow.
Everything used to be like a wall.
Everything used to, yeah, everything used to.
Now it's strange.
I'm not a kid anymore.
Sad more often than not.
No back—up, just me.
Even though now its orange
I am stating to see,
I'm the back-up for my kids.
I'm the yellow, I'm the wall.

It takes more tears when there is no back-up.
There is just me and I am their wall,
pray to God I don't fall.

# ACHE

Inside I ache.
This moment I dwell in tears.
Torn apart by a dream that lingers forever...
Forever beyond my grasp.
Sometimes I am ripped and shredded by emotions,
Thrust down deep into this sad place of sorrow.
And I know why.

I know why.

This yearning courses through me.
This longing for love.
My heart never finds solace in other's arms.
And I know why.

I know why.
As my tears run rivulets down my face in the odd hours.

I see that place everywhere.
I see it in others.
I see it in the sky,
In the dark,
In the trees.
And I hear whispers of love,
Secretly beckoning me on the teasing winds.
That place of love,
That elusive place.

I ache.
And I know why.
My desires never finding all encompassing future.
My searching, always searching,
Infinite desolate streets,
The voids of many false avenues.

And Oh God, I am torn apart mercilessly.
Lacerated by pain and craving.

I know why.
And I crawl on my knees, tears flowing like summer rain.
And I hurt.
Yes, I hurt.
The dream stays forever beyond my grasp.

I release love through my tears.
It is all I have.
That elusive place always hidden from my heart.
I ache and dream.
It is all I have.
Tears in the oddest hours.

# AIR

Help me catch my breath, you are my air.
I am standing here, introspection like slow fire.
Stay beside me forever.

In the night I suffered this scary thought that you left me and
disappeared.
My heart forgot how to beat.
My soul curled up in a corner like a forgotten cobweb.
My eyes, like an infinite waterfall, cascading tears.

This love that I have found with you lives inside me now.
A permanent part of my existence.
You are my quilts, cover me up and keep my heart warm.

Every second that we are apart, every minute away from you,
every hour, inside I shiver.
Envelope me and look at me with eyes that love me.

Every time we have touched...our love grows...
Every year we will blossom.
Hold me every night like I am your life.
Help me catch my breath, you are my air.

I breathe you in.
You are my air.

# ALWAYS

*The rest of my life was born in august of '98...*
*In the frozen blue eyes of you .*

*I walked slowly in a pasture on an autumn afternoon,*
*Feeling the soil beneath my feet, the sky overhead vast and immense.*
*And I existed in dreams that you embodied.*
*Clover and brown grass touched by soft breezes,*
*Like your kisses upon my skin.*

*I loved you before we ever met.*
*I dreamed of you my entire life.*
*I hoped and longed for the epitome of life's existence to appear.*
*I stood in many Texas pastures waiting for you.*

*Winter's rainy cold chill splatters on the windows.*
*I watch individual droplets race in rivulets down the glass.*
*I exist in the dream of you, each splatter of water,*
*a kiss from your serious soul.*

*I share my vulnerability with you.*
*I am nothing, I am everything.*
*I am only here to experience our world,*
*Together always, following our dual visions and goals,*
*Into summer sunsets, chasing dreams into spring fields of Indian*
*paintbrushes,*
*Searching for each other's smiles in the brisk cold of freezing fronts from*
*the winter.*
*Hand in hand striding forth in the fallen leaves of autumn.*

*Each year our destiny draws us into a vortex.*
*Each month we strive to complete the circle.*
*Each week we yearn to survive the longing of our hearts.*
*Each day we cry out across the separation, in desperate silent screams*
*of ache.*

*Each hour and minute our souls yearn to live freely, without constraint,*
*In harmonious, glorious rapture of the duality of our souls as ONE.*

*In the frozen blue eyes of you I see secret worlds where your love dwells.*
*In my light brown eyes I open up my worlds to your heart.*
*In the summer of '98 the rest of my life was born.*
*And I continue to follow my heart into uncharted worlds,*
*The infinite future of me and you, Gayln and Doug Hiser.*

*Strawberries and roses, parking lots and parks,*
*Soccer fields and pastures, locker rooms and living rooms,*
*White zin and hot tea, water bottles and chocolate milk,*
*Fingers entwined, tears shared, the treasure of a soulmate's embrace,*
*And we love like we have never loved before.*
*We love like destiny. We fulfill. We complete. We belong.*
*Together. G and D..........always,*

# BLUR

In the silence of a quiet house by the still water of the gulf,
I reflect with tears wetting my cheeks as I look out a cold
window.

What ever happened to truth, honesty, and morals?
Questions that blur the subconscious.
Words only, not substance or reality.

So I swim away in a dream of the white picket fence.
And I fly away with smiles in a fantasy of true love.
And I climb higher in a daydream of happiness and loyalty.
And I dream always of the dreamer's truth.

There is a dark sky of stars that millions have cast dreams
upon.
I cast mine among them once again.
I pray and cast my dreams away into the night,
Guided by my honest tears and my devoted emotions.

The corner of the room is a safety haven for my heart.
And the beer dulls my senses so that sometime before dawn...
I can drift into a dreamless sleep.

# Camouflage

I'm not the hero in every scene.
I could be but I'm not.
I hate to lose, but I can gracefully.
I can disappear into a jungle.
Wrap myself up in intermingled vines.
Tangle my heart with the inextricable forest growth.
Camouflage my hurt in desperate actions.

When this world wants too much.
My stomach has this empty space.
And this man that stands tall upon a hill,
questions God, questions Fate.
My soul cries like a lost swan without his mate.

I found what I sought.
This pot of gold.
This secret treasure behind the gate.
I discovered paradise.
An oasis, a haven, the lost world.
A place where I could survive, live forever.

Every road I traveled led to her.
And these tears won't stop.
I must be this silly fool.
To drown in the tear's pool.
To dwell in such highs,
and to lie here on an empty couch and die,
a thousand deaths.
A death a minute.
Each kiss like a scary truth.
My future uncertain.
Because every road leads to her.
And lying isn't my way.

There are angels on earth and I found one.
Her wings are tied by wicked circumstance.
A circumstance that I cannot live with.
A serious wrong.
A betrayal of my heart, my love.

Those blue eyes that melt me.
Those blue eyes that singe my soul.
Those same blue eyes that send bolts of fiery pain.

All I wanted  was to live forever in her arms.
All I wanted was her love.
Reality soaks me like gasoline.

Please don't drop that match.

# DEPTH

Remember always we are lovers and friends.
My love is infinite.
I didn't know the depths we could go.
So now I drown.

# Effervescence

This is my effervescence.
My vitality of existence.
I remember the softest touch of one finger,
on an August summer night.

Mysterious movements of shadows within us,
shaped our futures, pulled us as one, towards...
this destination upon this planet.
You revealed your soul, those frozen blue eyes,
piercing into me,
exposing this hidden heart.
I stood naked and vulnerable, before you,
awaiting the next move, knight to king,
checkmate.

As I hold you each day.
Precious touch.
You fill me with illuminating warmth.
As I love you with the infinite boundaries of myself,
I fall deeper into the chasm that is you.

I followed the Herculean force towards my future.
Dancing in your eyes like a graceful dove in the clouds.
I dance in the introspective moments of our courtship.

I drift away in your arms, standing by the water.
I swim within your eyes, in candlelight.
I shiver to think of washing your skin, in rose petals and
bubbles.
I tremble at thoughts of parking lots and parks,
sweet kisses of honey and sweat, wine and strawberries.
I exist only for you.
My life to bring smiles to your lips, your heart, your soul.

You are my effervescence.
You are my vitality of life.
I climb these empty rooms like a dreamscape.
Images of you adorn each wall.
Our destiny shaped by the shadows we contain.
The moon's pull on the water within us.
The sun's illumination radiating on our skin,
the way your kisses touch my heart.
When I swim in your frozen blue eyes,
I am complete.

The coldness in my stomach is the shadow...
the Fate pulling us together,
forever and ever.
This is my effervescence.
My love flowered and nourished,
in parking lots and parks.
I swim within your eyes, in candlelight.
I will never question our destiny.
My tears pure emotion to meld with your secret heart.
Our hearts that searched these many years.
Always somehow moving towards each other,
without knowledge of the other.
Only the dream.
Only the soul's longing to propel us upon this destined journey.

In parking lots and parks.
Roses and strawberries.
Kisses like honey and wine.
The softest touch of one finger,
one look and I knew my future.
I knew our dream stretched out before us.

To be complete we move forward,
led by the hand of Destiny,
following our hearts,
and the softest touch of one finger,
I remember, on an August summer night.

# Elusive Realm

Seduction.
That elusive realm.
Guided by my heart into flame.
The face of her, those eyes,
blue of arctic ice.
Frozen.

My indomitable journey through uncharted landscapes of
invective circumstance,
far away places, my resilient heart tested at every turn in these
infinite roads.
The roads of my future.

Should I wait for you?
Should I pour into you?
Should I stop my quest at your door?
Questions that have no need of answers.
The story has already begun.
I am delving into this lava, this road that turns and twists.
I am ready for fire.
For hurt or healing.
Into those blue eyes,
the eyes of arctic ice.

I am ready for all of this.
A leviathan love straining.
A universe spinning in this itinerant soul.
I feel like I am a gliding dragonfly, circling her like she is
quenching water.
I have a lavish piece of paradise.
I feel like I am an otter, swimming beneath the clear water
entwined with her.
I yearn for the beloved smiles of Eden.
I am ready for all of this.

Into those blue eyes,
the eyes of arctic ice.
I can see far out into the frozen horizon.
And she is always omnipresent.

Seduction.
That elusive realm.
True love.
Two hearts.
I will never be the same.
I see now.
Blue eyes of my future.

There I was, time had slipped by,
weeks ago.
I saw her flying by.
Blonde hair, streaming behind her, like a flag in smooth wind.
Lightning in her legs.
Grace in those little strides,
like a gazelle on the run.
I saw her spirited quickness, that lithe form flying.
I saw competitive intensity to match my own.
She has never left my sight.
In my sky, my nights, my soul remembers her every move.
Those blue eyes,
merging with mine in deepening affirmative moments.
Ice blue landscapes carry me away, in my dreams.

I am ready for all of this.

So I stand on a floral  hill.
I watch her precious face in the floating clouds.
I am barefoot, bare soul.
My heart, open to her.
Consumed with that explicit glimpse.
I smell the thunder in the sky, the rain far away.
The breeze brushes tears from my eyes.

I stand there.
Breathing.
I am alive.
I am ready for all of this.

This story has begun.
Twin souls finding each other,
in this vast sea of zillions.
The stars call out our names.
Each night  I look up from my place by the water.
I hear whispers of the vision.
And I breathe.
Frozen into the same ice as you.

We sat together in such a perfect time.
I could feel all into you.
I hold onto you.
And I am ready for all of this.
That elusive realm of Gayln.

# Tropical Mind

Splattering staccato droplets like burning carnality.
I plunge into unheard of depths, pure adrenaline, exotic inhalations.
Creepy crawler, sleepy baby, open your eyes and dance with me.
Take a chance.
With me.

So I stare at you through purple.
So I dare you to eat and bite with me.
So I desperately dream of uninhibited white light.
The sensation of time and the touch of intense pleasure fills.
Me up.

Exasperation like perspiration on my cheek.
Clues to the dark future like pawns on a chess board.
I dive through clear sheets into clouds that float in my bedroom.
Flying like a porpoise through thick air.
I take chances.
The risk.

All at once the tornado whirls around my skin.
And I die only to breathe a new oxygen.
And I soar like a sax bellow.
To die like this is metaphoric.

Each day of milk and roses we read every word.
Transmitted by excessive information stunting nature's reality.
There is a place where sky and sea meet.
A place of tranquility, a place of lakes and trees,
A place to be.
Tropical paradise of the mind is here.
In me.

So follow me sweetie baby.
Take a step into realms of roseate spoonbills, white egrets, cumulus clouds, red painted sunsets, white sugar sands, saguaro cactus, redwoods, inextricable vines, phosphorescent caves, tiny bats, secret waterfalls, pebble strewn creeks, rushing white water rivers, a dual rainbow between the mountains, the myriad multi-colored denizens of the coral reef, take a chance, follow risk become one with the reality of the true existence.

Love with truth.
With me.

# THE FORGOTTEN BOY

 I am the forgotten boy.
Tight sinew and blonde leather steel.
The tears of morning, the thunder rumbling in my sleep thoughts.
This numb waking,
accident of dreaming...stumbling like a primordial ancestor,
remembering how to feel, like I just got home from some infinite intoxicated vacation into realms of fantasy and forgotten emotions.

Whistling birds, screaming cartoon silhouettes, drinking hot tea in China, cascading my sadness into colored shapes and putting reality into a crayon box.
Vermilion banner, scarlet bookmark, written words of obscurity.
72 colors of sadness.
Drink it up boy!
Page after page .
stay in the lines.

The deepest Hendrix sky whispers yearning,
subconscious ultra-rendezvous with a demon of desire.
My brethren mock my form in shapes of twisted pretzel shadows.
I stand alone on the isolated brink of a brilliant seductive intensity.
A tear threatens to drop.

I am the forgotten boy.
Genetic link.
Page after page.
Unanswered inquiry.
72 colors of sadness.
Orphan boy blending,

whirling, turning, dancing, clenching, eating up syrup like a vacuum monster machine malevolent three mouthed mutant man standing at the apex of love and lust,
questioning embryonic evolution.
Questioning birth.
Procreation.

Moisture in my eyes.
Must be the humidity.
I am the forgotten boy.
A tear threatens to drop.

# HOME

This is a midnight ninja love,
secret of a sort.
This beautiful true love,
behind the waterfall.
I want to stand in the sun.
Raise my arms to the morning sky.
To bask in my home forever.

Clandestine kisses under stars and purple ceilings,
touching souls in a perfect pairing of two.
And in my heart I say "I do."
And I smile with you in my arms all the way through.

Our nights should never end.
Wrongful curfews casting shadows.
Our hands unclasping, our lips parting,
as you drive away ,
again.

When we can feel the morning together,
warmth fills the secret love behind the waterfall.
When we live in the light,
we shall merge and have it all.
I will be your name.
And you will be my heart, my air,
you will be my home.

# HYDRA

It is like it used to be.
The colors swirl in my eyes.
I reach out for the stability of your caress.
It doesn't exist.

The tears that are cold rivulets remind me of what you used to be.

I learned to endure pain.
I swam in emotions.
I lapped up your discarded kisses,
like a starving mongrel.
My eyes like sad pools filled with murky water.

I remember changing my clothes.
Changing my mercurial thoughts.
I move like clouds in the slowest sky.
I weep like a school boy in muddy new shoes.
It is like it used to be.

Vacant playgrounds.
A desert wasteland for my yearning.
I can see the spikes on the cactus.
Drip drop, drip drop, my blood pooling around my heart.
Each deed, word of hurt from your mouth, mind.
In my memory I need it to be the same.

I ate those lies.
I wanted lies.
I want what you used to be.
What you used to be.

In my dreamer's sleep, skin against skin, whispered words of
what I used to believe.

So I dream epic adventures into what you used to be.
I rescue you from hideous fire-breathing hydras, escape the claws of the humongous
lobster creatures, dash into the danger of the monster with dagger teeth, fight for you against the dreaded slasher bugs, attack hordes of evil poison walking plants, dive into the depths to pull you from the massive jaws of octopi-jellyfish-manta ray, and I still go back into the scary pits of lies for you.
Just to remember what you used to be.

Just to remember why this introspection still makes me cry.

I recline on this floor.
I put my fingers in my hair.
My eyes stare out of the window.
Rain splatters the glass.
Each water droplet mirrors your face.
My naked skin feels cold on the floor.
As if I could feel anything except this memory.
Of years ago.
There is wine and roses and candle light.
I creep alone with memories ,.,.,
I creep alone.
I want what you used to be.
What you used to be.

Years ago.
Hydra.

# I AM WIND

The wind caressed our skin
as we held each other
in the embrace of spirit and love.
Our lives entwined through fate and destiny,
Our thoughts merging together,
growing like ivy on the fence.
Each day we grow closer and hungrier.
Our spirits yearn to reach out and touch,
Across the circumstance that plagues us.

When I look deep into your eyes
I read your emotions.
And I still feel intense pain
at the wonder of YOU holding back,
That treasure,
that gift we both have for each other,
Your love.
Love that dominates
your entire soul constantly.
Our love that fills us daily,
gives us new reasons to strive for a future.

I am in a whir.
I am in a spiral.
I am cataclysmic incarnate.
I am submerged into a realm
of the purest emotion.
I can touch my heart with your finger.
My chest bare and open,
Vulnerable heart exposed
For pain and pleasure,
Touch me gently.
Hold me always.
Smile for me wherever you are,

and always know that my love for you
never, ever ends.

Like the wind caressed our skin,
I am caressed by these powerful emotions
that you have brought to life.
I am new and reborn and thrilled
And surprised and overwhelmed
And sensate and calm and nervous
And serene and scattered
trepidation and ravaged
and enlightened and confused
and valiant and persistent
and I will stay here for you.
I will be like wind.
ever blowing in your thoughts,
caressing you from the inside out.
And every time you feel a gust of wind,
know that it is my love
following you into your future.

OUR love grows like ivy on the fence.
inextricable vines entwining
and germinating.
Sprouting new vines that entangle,
twisting all our love
in a ever blossoming future.
We wont be able to see the fence...
someday ...
Our love dominating the fence,
climbing and growing everywhere.

I am the wind in your hair.
In your heart.
We are the ivy on the fence.
And we grow forever.

# IF I COULD SLEEP

If I could sleep for years I would desperately swim in a hidden secret lagoon with you.
Shades of exotic blue surrounding us like whispers of luscious intensity.
The sky merging with the sea as we climb into one another's skin.
Emotions scattered upward like a rainbow.
Inspiration is your love poured.
Like bubbles and clouds.

Inside your heart I would dwell in a bound trance of devotion.
Cascading when I feel your touch.
Call my name with each gasp of breath.

Captured by infinite passion I roll around the floor naked.
I keep you within my eyes.
I caress G and A and Y and L and N.
My aim is straight and seductive like swirling caramel.
The shower pours water on the serious mermaid goddess.

I step back and watch the water puppy play.
Bubbles.
If I could spin upside down like a whirling twister I would spin around your soul.
Each spiral of wind is my extension of steadfast loyalty.
Craving filling the belly of love.

Smothered by eternal lacerations of sugar stripes on my neck.
I cry like a lost child whimpering in the desert.

The ceiling becomes my panoramic view of life.
Praying like a monk in a casket of sleep I close my eyes in reverence.
And I wonder.

About bubbles, and sleep, and kisses like honey accompanied by stings from the flying wasps, and nightmares of near death on sharp nails, and hidden agendas, cranky porch inhabitants, the color that isn't a color, voids of non-existence, zoning, 31 ice cream salons, and I wonder.
I wonder about surface and about the river, and about the depths yet to delve within her.
So I dream of blue and the ocean is our home.

In my dreams the water puppy plays.
And I always dream of holding hands in the sea.
Craving forever filling our belly of love.
And I dream of expectations.
 Fulfilled with scintillating consequence.
We walk together into a sunset.
A silhouette of two souls joined at the heart

If I could sleep...

# In my life

This morning waking up to beauty I long to kiss her eyes.
Late at night I feel all into her and we sit together by the water.
Drinking beer and wine like clouds in a clear sky.
I reach out and touch her leg.
Heaven.

Heaven just to be in her life.

My thoughts all day at work turn to those eyes.
Tattoo a searing message on my heart.
Forever is what those scribbled words jot down across the page.
I reach out to hold her hand.
Pleasure.

Pleasure just to be near her.

When we are apart I feel like a lone swan swimming.
A solitary wanderer in search of sustenance.
Pouring down emotions like scattered storms on a sunny day.
I stand closer to her with my hand on her shoulder.
Warmth.

Warmth to merge with her.

Slow, fast, careful, risky, loving, frisking, touching, feeling, talking, kissing, biting, searching, twisting, cascading, hugging, sharing, rolling together like a tornado.

The day we met I remember her first words, "We need to talk."
And she remembered my first words, "This is for you."
She is the best I will ever live.

I give my best to her.
My beauty.

Beauty resides in our relationship.

Special moments, pile up, one after the other.
And we live and love through it all.
Life here is survival and we endure.
Two hearts with constitution.

We sit outside drawing closer.
Winding down each night in an embrace and a clenched sleep.
We dream and stay close in midnight spoons.
And life is here.
Life.

Life is here with her.
Always.

# LIKE ALL TRUTH

Aromatic remembrances of kaleidoscopic integration and I can
see
With my vision from deep within my tortured and devoted
heart...
I still dance on my carpet with her.
She is always here like a serious shadow following me room to
room.
So we dance an estranged waltz, and I melt once again into her.

I watch the coruscating sunset spraying rays of hot color into
the dragon's clouds.
I tip my cowboy hat to the setting brilliant orb and tenderly
wink at the horizon.
I recline and dwell upon the last gentle touch of her fingers on
my skin.
I dance again with her by the water, a wisp of a silhouette
outlined in my empty embrace.
I melt once again into her.

*A solitary soul wandered an emotional vastness like a desert refugee*
*And the internal damage refused to heal for so many years.*
*A loving heart persevered without sustenance*
*Like a cactus growing lonely without spines for defense.*
*The spirit yearned and dreamed and searched without a map,*
*Without a clue, without a guide, without guarantees*
*And like all truth ...*

Melts. Merges. Love.

Spiritual love lives beneath the skin, in the deep core of a
being.
Lifetimes may pass and never find the everlasting truth.
One day I melted.
I danced in dreams.

I found the beginning.
I found my lifetime stretched out before me in her eyes.
And like all truth...

I melt each time,
With her.

# Majestic Place of the Sea

It was you who brought me here.
*Sweet kisses like honey on your lips.*
To this majestic place of the sea.
You found me in the unfathomable water, deep and frantically struggling.
I reached for your captivating heart, clinging and holding.
Breathing you in.
*Our love goes on.*

Look in my devoted eyes and see into me.
Our love is there.
I will be protector, guardian, safe keeper,
wizard, lover, husband,
I will be there for you always.
Breathing you in.

Years will go by.
Our love will multiply.
True love is ours.
Pure love is our shadow.
The moon will know our silhouette.
The sun will kiss our skin.
*Our love goes on.*

I will be there for you.
When the night comes I will be wrapped around you.
When the morning silently creeps into our room,
I will ardently kiss your eyes awake.
When you cry I will hold you.
When you laugh I will smile.
There will always be a fervent light in my eyes.
A light in my heart for you.
*Our love goes on.*

We dream  consummately together.
We walk perpetually together.
Fly together, soaring into the zenith of our love.
Kissing with luxurious sparks, embracing in an electric touch.
Locking eyes in our eternal loving vision.

I am the otter.
You are my playmate.
We swim in the sea.
The sea of our love.
*Our love goes on.*

I sleep curled embryonic around your warmth.
We will never be lonely.
We will always be the half of our whole.
To hurt me is to hurt you.
To hurt you is to hurt me.
I breathe you, you breathe me.
Our love goes on.
Twin hearts, dual souls, two become one.
Our love goes on.
This majestic place of the sea.

Sweet kisses like honey on your lips.

# MONDAY MORNING

Standing next to a second story window, wrapped in a familiar old quilt,
I stand and stare at the rooftop.
Seven seagulls land all in a row.
My tears caress my face like cold penguin kisses.

I can see a Monday sky in the early morning.
I can feel so much, so deeply into the morning.
And the mourning, the sadness mingles with the uncertainty.
Now I watch neighbors across the water.
They cast lines for fish, have their morning coffee,
reading newspapers on wooden decks, the clouds above us all.

I stand alone, my face to the glass,
tears blurring the window.
I am warm in my quilt.
My heart is warm with far away love.
So I wait.
I wait.

I wait for the tears to stop.
I wait for the sobs to dissipate.
My hair is tangled.
My fingers clench tightly my quilt,
wrapped around me like a safe cocoon.
I am alone.

At the window.
Of the world.

I wait.
For her.

# November Second-Water Train

November second.
Six o'clock full moon,
like the white virtuous eye of a malamute.
The surreptitious woods like a valid extension of my aura,
all around rapturously seeping into me.
We stand alone on a bridge.

You stand behind me.
I can still feel your enchanting hands encircling me,
warmth envelopes my skin, my heart beats
the syllables of your name.
Our souls embrace in nature,
in this dusk time, on this structure,
above dark water.

I am real and alive when we live our promises.
I stand holding you like extinction.
A water train of geese appear magically beneath us,
like an ecstatic omen of the future traveling before us.
So I dream of wild kisses.
My skin alive with you inside of me like bright fire.
Desire.

Our hands clasp so naturally.
Our lips yearn.
Our emotional duality.

I travel in your eyes.
I travel in your touch.
And I dream of our life.
Walking beside you into a hidden lagoon.
Swimming in clear waters beside you like mythical merfish.
My arms about you in a phosphorescent secret cave.
Standing beside you, wind in our hair,
at the pinnacle of a craggy peak.

Your pure fragrance in my memory like a my own name.
I travel with you always.
Infinity, luscious journeys, delicious forays,
internal intimacy, external merging, and we have become one.

The geese swim away in the water train.
We stay always in our eternal embrace.
And the November full moon watches,
like the white eye of a malamute.
The dark water stares back at us,
mysteries of our future.

I drive away with my dreams alive inside.
I drive away and your eyes are before me.
I dream of reclining in pastures of sweet clover with you.
I yearn to climb towers of rocks to find a lost stream with you.
I dare dream to hold you forever.
I dare to dream to fly into your arms each night.
I dare to be your prince.
I will be everything you could ever dream.

Candle light fills our souls.
We  taste of each other's wine,
intoxicating.
Intoxicating just to breathe with you.
I dream of your heartbeat.
The calmest quiet in the sky.
Your heartbeat next to mine.

We stood alone on a bridge.
November second.
The dark water's unknown depths.
Contemplating fate.
The only known truth,
you and I.
The earth's silence gave many signs.

Destiny's eye, the full moon.
The water train of geese, our streaming future.
A climbing raccoon, escalating emotions.
The second trail back, a new beginning.
The earth's silence, our dreams.

I will always remember the water train.
I dare to dream.
And we shall never wake.
Wild kisses.
Honey and nectar.
My shoulder, your pillow each night.
I listen to your heartbeat,
the calmest quiet in my sky.
Your heartbeat next to mine.

# Our Truth of Habitat

Each time I look at you, each time...
It is like a child looks at Christmas morning.
Each time I gaze deep into your eyes, each time...
It is like diving from a cliff into azure water.
And I feel your name in my heart.
And I roll your name around inside my mind like a chocolate kiss...
Savored in my mouth.

When I am left alone at night I create visions of you on the ceiling.
When I cannot close my eyes I roam our memories.
When I toss in tangled sheets, when I thrust my hands in tangled hair,
When I nervously twist my hands, when I dream scary dreams,
I seek sanctuary in our truth.
I seek protection in the love that dominates my heart.

Each time I gently kiss your lips, each time...
I feel the warmth of showering, tepid water upon my head,
Cascading down my spine, rivulets of pleasure upon my skin.
Each time I am near you, your fragrance, the scent of you fills me, each time...
It is like tropical gardens filled with hummingbirds dancing,
Flitting about the exotic aromas of a multitude of resplendent flowers.
And I fly across chasms on the smooth wings of our love.
And I dream of a day where the black and white world of Kansas
Transforms into the living color of Oz...
Our habitat of true love.

# Restless Tranquility

The mist in my eyes blurs my eternal craving.
*Such sweet moisture with immense power.*
Standing under an ancient tree, a timeless representative of the cycle of life.
A centurion guarding one place on the earth.
I can feel so much in this moment, tremendous spatial delving into an arena of secret awareness.
Such a restless tranquility, as if I am nature itself, a manifestation of every particle,
Pouring from my earth mother's DNA,
The offspring of the genetics' of EVE.

I can feel the obtrusive grooves and celestial wrinkles of age in the coarse bark.
I feel livid scars upon my own inner flesh, the searing pain
And the overwhelming cascade of my most precious love.
A love that surrounds my soul in a beautiful wardrobe.
At that instant a ladybug flits around the flowers and lands gently upon my arm.
A shiny red sphere of a beetle, a metaphor for a tiny scarlet heart.
And I watch her crawl with tickling steps and I daydream hidden desires.
She tires of the journey upon me and launches into a haphazard flight.
*And the tree whispers a name to me.*

I tremble as each syllable soaks into my skin like humidity.
The primordial tree's leaves sing her name with help from the wind.
And I am swept away into a state of ephemeral being that flies across the uncountable voids,
I am away from my human body, a place of souls and purity.
*Finding the celestial heaven of true love.*

I turn and spin like a whirlwind but yet I am the center,
Becoming a calm within chaos.
My true heart emoting the flame of love and hurricane of passion.
Colors melt my wet eyes until I see only far away.
Far away where her blue eyes dominate the sky.

The mist in my eyes blurs my eternal craving.
I satiate the river of flow.
I cry too much.
I love more than desire.
I wish always.
I dream the future.
And my words pour like all environmental existence.

*Breathe.*

Hugging this tree I can feel life.
And it starts to rain.
Rivulets of water down the trunk,
The lifeblood of the mother earth.
And my tears blend with the blood of mother earth.
And I see her in the distance.
Walking like an ethereal spirit towards a collision with destiny's granite stone.
She merges with the rock, and I slip into the bark.
Soil marries wood and stone in a shifting of elements,
On comes the massive upheaval of power and magic that defies logical parameters.

We breathe as one entity, the breath of the silence of discovery of love and chemistry.
*We breathe.*

# Rivers

I cry rivers.

In my darkest dreams I scatagory, clambatory screech inside out.

Enthralled by viscous surreally beckoning without abandon,

I reach out from dreamland azure.

My fingers absurd television antennae curiously searching for her flesh.

So I swim the languid streams of the sky and I drown in her name.

This is my world of origin.

My creation of existence, piquant and quaint, bulbous and ridiculous,

It is this place of longing and futuristic dynamics.

Crawl to me on your hands and knees.

Supplicate yourself and bind your wrists with an overpowering love.

I am entwined by emotion, wrapped in Houdini chains by my heart.

This drink of mine is potion and poison and delicious and addicting.

This bottled fountain of purity.

Tiny piano notes embalm us in the naked place of skin.

I cry rivers to exist here with her.

When she embraces me={{ *totalitarian distance livid lust albino thrust licking sensuous exasperation purple rhythm supersonic orgasmianism delving*}}

baby oh baby>>>>delving into new arenas.

Brand spanking new and improved places of the heart.

In my darkest dreams I always surface to Gayln's face.

Dreams left behind for those eyes.

Her soul beckons mine.

I cry rivers to exist here in this lifetime with her.

# Silhouette

In the hidden violet night I walk alone under the serenity of the moon.
I walk alone with my heart soaring across the Heaven's, searching for her.
The stars are my teardrops upon her shimmering skin when we kiss.
The luscious breeze her fingertips on my arm as I remember how we first touched.
And I am a solitary waiting silhouette, filled with the vastness of pure love,
Infinite emotion, and the eternal devotion to my princess who lives so far away.

I am a barren ground.
A desert.
Wasteland.
A wounded husk, hollow inside like a hive,
Without the stings or the buzz.
I am the solitary waiting silhouette.
I am the Love that waits.
I am her love.

And without her I am the empty vessel.
I wait for my moments.
Each moment I breathe with her ,
I am the ocean's crashing waves on boulders.
Each moment I dwell in silence and solitude,
I am the tide pool isolated from the sea.

I am the Love that waits.
And I have found that I have no answers.
I have no limit to pain.
I have only heart beats for her.
I am the solitary waiting silhouette.
I live the war between hurt and love.

Love.
Checkmate.

# SMOOZIE

Landing together ... as we kiss like a smoozie.
 I will kiss you from out of the entire space that separates our entities.
I will promise to touch all  into you.
Seeing signs along the neon highway that traverses mountains, streams of rippling fire, desire like invisible ghosts of lust.
Staccato tongue, liquid arrangements into whirlpools of orgy dust.

Wild eyed doe girl creeping like a smoozie.

Be there or be chaired.
I will promise blood from my wrist veins.
Guitar string broken diamond vow chocolate party luscious guilt behind closed eyes.

Do I like to dream.
Like visionary epitome.
There was this tree.
This simple bark-less tree.
One tree standing like solitude.
Like old age .
Like serenity and secrecy.
There I stood before the tree.
This ancient tree bringing my mind into the marrow of pulp and sap and photosynthesis.

Walk into me.
Is it safe?
Yes.
Is it safe?
No.
Get down on your knees.
Leave me ...never.

I promise to touch  all into you.
My kiss from within your bark-less soul.
Your hand on my exterior.
Your hand, my branch.
your branch, my hand.

We are leaves.
And we fly and float on autumn breezes.
Touching as we land together on the ground.
As we kiss.

# Summer Night in July

There is only you in my heart.
Surrounded by the remembrance of your sweet whisper to me,
I immerse my yearning soul and reach out to the majestic night
sky so far above me.
I recline here by calm water beneath the myriad stars extant in
your eyes
As they float before me filled with tears of the purest love.
Touch me... from far away.

This utopian paradise we have discovered embraces like the
warmth of family.
Our secret grotto beckons us forward into each other's arms.
Look into my deep brown eyes and see what heartening smiles
await you.
Search my thoughts to find only infinite love flows.
You are my cosmos, my galaxy, my universe,
My fingers stretch to find your skin,
And the touch of you that completes me each time.

There is no other for me.
There isn't any different life for me to lead.
There is only you in my heart.

Discover, day after day, the truth of what I stand for.
Some might say a white night in shiny armor.
Some might say a cute couple we make.
Some might say destiny led us together.
What some might say matters not.
Simple truth is absolute.
Simple truth walks with us hand in hand,
Truth is,
We love.

We love.
There is no other for me.
There isn't any different life for me.
There is only you in my heart.


I wake up disoriented in time, missing you, in the dreaming nights.
I gasp and struggle with tangled sheets.
I need your serious blue eyes and your tranquil heart next to me.
When you are here I am a gentle heartbeat for your pillow.
I will always be the serenity in your life,
The constant you can depend on,
The reliable trust that follows you like a comfortable secure shadow.


I wake up from a dream you are curled up in my arms once again.
The quiet night reminds me of our love.
And I sleep again in your arms, your hair on my shoulders like the softest silk.
With your head on my chest, your heart beats in time with mine.
Your soft breathing brings the placid water's calm to our sleep.


There is no other for me.
There isn't any different life for me to lead.
There is only you in my heart.


On my knees, my hands forming the church,
And the steeple, I remember you showing me,
All the people.
Our love, so pure and destined, is our church.
God watches over the truthful.
That mysterious power that resides within us is a gift from Heaven.
So we both hold hands on the edge of the chasm of the future.

Each moment we have shared becomes another sealed book of photos.
Our memories like fields of flowers in our minds.
Springtime in our life has arrived.

Love almost passed us by.
So we say our prayers at night with enfolded hands like a church.
And we cry tears of happiness looking into each other's eyes.
Love found us.
We love.
When you are gone I am only half.
When we enfold our union melds like two droplets of rain become one.
Best friends, intense lovers, reservations for double occupancy,
Do not disturb.

# The Poster Boy

The sound of tires crunching on a quiet road ...
fade into the distance as she disappears.
This was a dream of reality.
I stand like a poster boy for black cowboy hats and tears.
A perfect picture for unbuttoned jeans, barefoot on cold concrete.

My fingers waved goodbye but my heart always says "hello."
My eyes can only see her each second that I exist.
I am a man on fire,
serious scorching,
holding a strait flush, betting the ranch...
frozen in time, waiting for the player to either raise me or call.

I turned off the porch light and just stood there,
staring at those red tail lights drive away.
Red lights, valentine's and hearts, deep red, scarlet, vermilion, cardinal, blood,
lights getting smaller and smaller, my dream almost out of sight.
I rest my head on my arms, powerful yet helpless.
A silent tear.

My door closes slowly, like some massive drawbridge closing up.
I immerse myself in the darkness of my stairway,
feeling how she must feel.
Knowing her pain, knowing her torment,
I plummet myself into her world and feel her pain.
Anguish in her veins.

The floor is cool on my feet.
I climb the stairs very slowly,
lost in thought.

Eerie shadows touch me as I step.
Shadows that soothe me and settle my soul.

I am the lost man.
I am the poster boy of the black cowboy hats and tears.
I am the king of love.
I am holding a strait flush, queen of hearts high.
Betting the ranch.
Win it all or lose everything.

I have never gambled much in my life.
It has never been my way.
And I stand before my open windows,
watching the rippling water of the canal.
AND all I can see is her eyes.

The eyes of my queen of hearts.
And my fingers waved goodbye but my heart always says,
"hello."

# The Secret of Love

*What if love is truth?*
*A situation of honesty and loyalty backed up against a wall of circumstance.*

*The children and the parents and the sisters and the brothers and the cousins*
*And the friends and the co-workers and everyone else are in a big circle.*
*Creating a large symbolic circumference of factors and an imitation of real life.*
*And the truth lies dormant and camouflaged like the fawn concealed from the leopard.*

*What if the fork of the road never goes away.*
*An indecisive moment that pauses time and catapults emotion*
*Into the fields of straw and long grasses.*

*An intravenous nerve shock.*
*A thank you from an enemy.*
*An "A" on your report card in Math.*
*A winning race, a finished marathon, and*
*Finding true love.*

*What if love is devotion and unwavering selflessness?*
*The serious delving of retrospection into the depths of a heart*
*Might be the final answer to love.*
*When my eyes close for the final time.*
*My passing from this life, let me be looking at you,*
*Gayln.*

*The secret of love is benevolence.*

# Trance Come To Me

She is my only truth.
The ocean of love.

I settle in to this emotion like the slow clouds over the ocean.
A vastness of purity fills me as I watch the life of the water.
I feel alone but connected to her always.
The ever-present sadness sometimes has its perverse way with
me.
But it is always last to love.

She is the water.
Mysterious.
Unpredictable.
Alluring.
Infinite.
She is my love.

Trance come to me.
A viable resolution will never be here.
This is my world of imperfection and illogical truths.
To try so hard is to expect results.
Results are fantasy.
Dancing in an ethereal place, an elusive zone of dreams,
Brings me closer to her.

I have always known I would wait forever...
When this mate of emotion walked into my soul.
To give of myself is natural.
To open, to expose, to be freely selfless,
Is to be honest to everyone including myself.

Trance come to me and bring my tears.
Cleansing thoughtful sadness, closer to the reality.
Dreams carried me this far,

Why give up on them now?
Trust in my heart.
It only hurts when I cry.

Slow clouds over the ocean.
The water moves with a life.
A life filled with emotion.
Tears of purity.
I love her.
I found out how to love with her.
She is my only truth.

# Treasured Embrace

This would be a lonely world without you, my love.
I couldn't even go from here to there without the thought of
you.
I couldn't fathom how to breathe, how to function, how to
exist
Without your treasured embrace to hold me.

If you ever disappeared, my world would be extinct.
Plants wouldn't grow, lightning wouldn't flash,
Sun wouldn't set, moon would stay hidden behind the
blackness
Of a starless sky.
If you ever disappeared, so would I.

You are the star that's shines brightly in my heart.
You are the clover that is gently to my tread.
You are the breeze that caresses my skin.
You are the epitome of all that I am.

My world wouldn't be a world without you.
I couldn't get from here to there, I couldn't exist in it
anywhere.
I couldn't go on without your kisses, your hugs, your loving
eyes.
I am all that I am just to be here to make you smile,
To be your other half, your loving man, your best friend.
I drown each night in the dreams of your love.
I dream of your treasured embrace.

# OTTERS

I hold my breath, not wanting to interrupt the dream.
The dream I have waited on and on and on, in this life.
I hold my breath.
I anticipate our merging like two otters in a clear cold stream.

Hundreds of flowers adorn our hearts.
Thousands of kisses linger in our souls.
I cry on my pillow`.
I clench my teeth in frustration and anger.
I shout out wild thoughts in an empty house.
I tenderly dwell in introspection,
So that I may learn from the memories.

The abyss lies before us.
The cosmos stretches out a trail of stars.
These roads both beckon intangible futures.
My eyes always search the sky.
Searching the sky for her eyes.

I follow her promises.
I believe in her.
My trust is my path.

We are two otters slinking, sliding,
Playing through life.

So I hold my breath.
And I love without limit.
And if I breathe at all,
It will be inhalation of you.

# TWO

*I devote my life to you.*
*Our song of two.*
In this alone realm of serious delving,
I search the depths of my purest love for you.
I find ultimate blessings.
I discover immaculate emotions.
I learn of the power of exquisite true love.
I learn how dominating my love for you is.
I devote my life to your happiness.

I recline here in darkness, without sleep.
Your face adorns the walls of my rooms.
Even with my eyes closed you are before my inner vision.
I have never swam in such deep water.
Gladly I drown in your soul.
I supplicate my heart and I hand you my life.

Tears come to me in this alone darkness.
Wetting my face and soaking my love.
A sheer film of liquid drenching my serenity.
I reach out of this darkness trying to find you.
I grasp air.
I long to feel your touch.
The taste of honey lingers from your kisses.
And I roll on the floor with the ghost of your memory.

Serious delving brings me closer to my lonely spirit.
These reclusive nights go on for many desperate hours.
Into your dreams I try to fly.
Reaching out from a distance to call your name.
God hears me crying.
My strength helps me in the darkness.
And I stare out the window at the waves of the water.
And I stare and see your eyes in the night sky.

You are my ultimate blessing.
Pain and pleasure, hand in hand.
The most difficult test of eternity.
*My trust is in us.*
This never ending saga of adversity and complication.

I discover the epitome of love.
The meaning of my life.
My surest destiny.
All that I yearn for resides within you.
We are special.
*We are a song of two.*
We are the results of a test.
I stand strong throughout these cruel infinite anxieties.

*I devote my life to you.*
*Our song of two.*

# Under the Mimosa

I stand in this southern Texas pasture,
in the tranquil shade of a Mimosa tree.
Pink blossoms like a pink flamingo sky above me .
I began to believe in fate.
Introspective moments while my questing heart beats.
Drifting, and I don't concentrate.
I fly away following your face in my inner vision.
I fly away on fire.

I am powerful in my invulnerability.
This strength of sinew and contained love...waiting.
To capture this dream .
To shed this shiny heavy metallic armor.
To exist so vulnerable in your arms.
Consumed by your hidden burn.
My little one, I yearn.

I can see our intimate embrace.
The moon watches from a secret sky.
Two shadows, two silhouettes,
become one under a Mimosa tree.

Tree of pink, in this landscape of the future,
in my vision, I  stand naked upon the tallest hill,
arms outstretched,
breathing in, breathing in,
Heaven.
You live inside me like destiny.

I see our embrace,
my kisses like thousands of droplets from a hidden waterfall,
electric drops splattering all over your skin.
Your loving heart filled with the deepest Earth's passion.
You travel.
Port Lavaca, Texas, to the tip of my life.

And I know you burn.
I know how your heat simmers inside of your soul.
I burn too.

If I knew where you live I would leave fresh picked flowers and jars of honey on your doorstep.

If I knew where you live I would decorate your house with brilliant scarlet hearts.

What is meant to be always finds a way.

I exist in this Texas pasture, my skin caressed by tall grasses as I recline.
Clover fragrance buzzing about me.
Floating clouds drifting slowly above, outline your face.
Your face in my sky.

I never question why.

You.

Your words reverberate wildly inside of me.
Piercing my world, transfixing me with luxurious portent.
Your words the luminous music of special syllables.
You are the lost treasure.
Your words fill me in my Texas pasture
and one tear slides slowly down my face as I dare dream.

I dream and I know you burn.
I guess at your depths.
How deeply you feel.
Under a Mimosa tree.
I know the heat you carry.
The fire under your skin.
The ocean's unquenchable surging love.

As the tides turn,
you burn.
And I have found you
because I burn too.

# Valentine Lemon Pie

On my night,
Delicate scissors-circling breasts,
The shredding of encumbering cloth,
Cutting away the inhibitions,
Revealing our luscious passion.

Merging like liquid lovers in a surreal darkness,
Climbing together to fevered heights,
We journey climatically and devour in pleasure on that first
night.

On your night,
Dimly lit table setting with teasing hands,
And anticipatory questing on an early night drive.
The tricky lust and the sweet love embodied between us
Like a blue flame inside my soul.

My hunger drives your car into neutral
As frenetic lovers we search for privacy.
Urgency leads me into a surprise!

The candles burn, flickering flames of expectation.
The room contains elements of true love, devotion, passion,
And an honest sweetness pervaded in each thoughtful act.
Wine in ice with chilled flutes, lingerie draped like a promise,
Treats and oils awaiting our tastes,
And the lovers reward, the sharing of our flesh and our souls,
And a lemon pie on the air conditioner.

Valentine's weekend two thousand,
Sunday morning we kiss like completion.
Braiding wet hair on the bed,
Coffee from the office, barefoot boy in the rain,
And the family at worship, all snug and close.

Your arm in mine in church,
The slight touching of our hands, our fingers,
And God watches us...
And smiles.

# Whale Song

Listening to whale cries from the far away sea,
in my mind, like sweet inundation.
I can feel their sorrow.
I can feel that delicious pain.
I can revel in the dark of my late night house.
*I search for the mirror within her.*
I revel in this torn atmosphere of my shredded soul.

It is like I float slowly within the depths,
glancing upwards towards the surface.
The sun's rays filtered through sea water,
camouflage pattern on the waves.
I am the serious mammalian, swimming through the water,
like a vessel of smooth gliding love.
And I cry my sorrow in the depths.
*My love that never dies.*
My all powerful love reaching ever upwards.
In search of.
In search of.

I sing the whale song.
I cruise in this sea of tears.
*Deeper and deeper I swim.*
Delving into my straining soul.
And there is nothing I can do,
but sing to her and cry for her,
*and love her always.*

So I listen to the whale song.
I feel all into this love.
*Understanding nothing.*
Patiently gliding in these dark depths,
catching glimpses of what my future,

will hold...wish to hold...want to hold...
*in search of.*
The mirror within her.

# Winds of the Tempest

The winds of the tempest pass by our years
Like eye blinks of the gods
And we will only remember the times we paused,
Looking back.

The speed of responsibility blinds our heart
And the weight burdens as if the sky were solid rock.
So I preach by the water and whisper into your ear
How our lives move forward and we lose precious days,
Precious memories, special moments lost to the speed
Of the wind of the tempest.

Months run into months like minutes,
And a few moments staring out across calm water
Seem to be only a breath in the cycle of love.

I once heard , "live each moment as if it were your last,"
And thought that extreme,
Until reality clenches life, and we see pain and fear in eyes of our
loved ones.

So I look back with tears in my eyes
At our tiniest moments that burn so brightly in my heart.
And I dream of more.
The winds of the tempest take away from us,
As month runs into month and each day is blown away
Like scattered dust on an old porch.

We always hope for more time the next day, the next week,
But I just continue to look in your beautiful eyes and dream of
time.
A time when the tempest has gone and we become our own
circle.

# Wink of an Eye

We live with our decisions for the rest of our lives.
We cry real tears.
We never except the pain with open arms.
I wish I were a wink of an eye.
My spirit that little flash of happiness.

I give my soul.
I expose my vulnerable heart.
I stand naked before her.
My tears like question marks in the sky.

My one and only denies my heart.
My other half turns the other cheek.
My true love has other loyalties.
My dream was just a dream,
that could have come true...
if reality was logical.

I believed everything.
I drowned in my emotions.
The sky beckons me to stand up...
to whisper prayers, to remember intimate moments,
and relive paradise.

I sit in disbelief.
In the web of desperate love.
A coldness cascading throughout me,
glacial ice of intensity, shredding my purest of thoughts.
I believed in everything.

I am a ghost .
A pirate.
A sailing ship lost in a storm.
A solitary lost swan.

My love for infinity...
isn't enough.

I believed in destiny.
Mr. Fate is cruel.
Someday I will die,
and my eye will wink.
And she will remember how much I loved her,
and no other.

# ANOTHER BEER

Those cackling crows come flapping,
intruding upon my quiet space inside this place.
The flames stretch out wavering hands skyward.
And the Devil's friend wants to come over for tea and cookies.

My fingers in my hair and I can't keep my eyes shut.
I hear their stupid laughter and feel their spit on my face.
Get those flapping feathers out of here.
I think I better get up and drink another beer.

Little Jack Horny sat in a corner,
masturbating with dirty fingers.
And that smart-ass spider filmed him from on top of the TV.

Every time I look up, this is all that I can see.
The weary grins of fat people and snobbish young girls,
driving the cars that Daddy bought.
I keep turning and those Baptists scream about the fire,
the Catholics complaining about fornication and evil desire.
And the Jehovah Witnesses just keep walking down Saturday
morning streets and waking the neighbors.

Those nights when sleep won't come and my head is alive,
I'm feeling shivers of heat or an icecube melting down my
spine.
In my dreams there is a victor and a monster, a wicked queen
and a beautiful slut.
And I always get the girl and end up changing the world.

Inside this place I can have no quiet when the crows nest
and cackle and the Devil's friend comes knocking.
So I lie back, rubbing my face and mussing my hair,
and then I get up and have another beer.

# COWBOY BOOTS

I learned to walk in cowboy boots
*found it made my legs sturdy*
Had a straw, broad-brimmed hat
*it was white with a red feather band.*

Chester was the name of my first horse
*He had a cotton stuffed head and a striped broomstick body*
A fast horse and he never bucked.

*Never really liked the cows like I should*
*Never took to the tobacco between my cheek and gum*
*I knew I never would.*

The cotton came out of Chester's head
Soon after he was dead.

*I would not be the right kind of cowboy*
*Those sad songs would always haunt me*
*Still do.*

But I learned to walk in cowboy boots
It made my legs sturdy.
My son is walking in cowboy boots
Walking in my boots, too.

I'm still not the right kind of cowboy...
*But I look good naked in cowboy boots.*

# DEEP RIVERS

And I am not what I seem.
And we are not what is seen.

The situations are not what they perceive.

She is not what she seems.
We are not what is seen.
And she is not what I have seen.
And we are not what we seem.

The circumstances are not what they feel.

But the blood flows in a secret river.
A deep river.
It never runs dry .
A river of blood, reflected in my eyes.

We are not as we are,
because of what we are,
and that is why we are,
and how we are, the way we're found  to be.
Not the way we long to be,
wish to be, want to be.
Yes...

Wish to be, want to be.
Wish to be, want to be.
Deep rivers, you and me.

# CHOCOLATE DUCK

The lovers were together on a bridge of wood.
Blue-gray civil war sky enveloping tiny moments.
Words of music passed from one to the other,
and a chocolate duck swam underneath.

Ripples of green-gray water ran from the duck.
Never once did he look back.

The lovers were together on a bridge.
Eyes of passion, and their skin as one.
Wine drained away.
Their restraints longed to be.
A chocolate duck swam as the ripples run.
They loved each other, the planet and the sun.

Love like a life, precious and cherished forever.

They kissed soft, exploring their held back emotions
They tested and felt.
They wanted and cried.
Strange hand that Fate had dealt.
And their time was up and they almost died...inside.

But in parting, a kiss.
Power and a tremendous emotion poured.
Sweet Heaven joined ultimate bliss.

And she went left, and waved good-bye.
And he went right, and felt as if he could fly.

And a chocolate duck swam down the bayou.

# DREAM OF THE LUSCIOUS JUMBLE

*Looking ahead for the fortunes of the future...*
I FOUND A PRINCESS JUST OUTSIDE MY DOORWAY.
Bits and pieces and unraveled string—something about her eyes,
her sensitivity, and then the JUMBLE BEGAN!

Lost in the marble of a crocodilian's eye,
swirling thoughts about that fucking scary place,
my future, the beyond.

And I was staring at her again,
captured by those twinkling gems,
tied up like Houdini in a thousand gallon tank.
Those bubbles, bubbles floating to that distant surface.
SEVEN-UP.

*Across the room, the dark room, there were fourteen pianos, all banging*
*away like ferocious gloved white fingers.*

*OH God...grunting like a wounded pig.*
*Kicked and then smashing a sharp iron spike in my heart.*
*Out of nowhere, out of the future.*
*The cock sucking present.*
*How bad can the future be?*
*Obscenely ominous.*

*The jumble rumbled on and on and on and on...*

I was pulsating, strobing in, throbbing and vibrating, jumping in
an electric trance, wicked the way she can make me go to sleep
without my lids moving. Sleeping in a velvet coffin wrapped up
in my future, in her, like some damn sex vampire that cannot be
killed.

My mild rage is aimed with deadly accuracy at the past and miss future wags a finger a me, a middle sarcastic finger.
And darling I am pissed off!

The princess of my soul, sucking me dry, like a green spider in a dewy web, sticky and tasty and heading for the center of my brain.
Mandibles destroying each cell like a cluster of juicy grapes.
Disregarding that terrible ache, that wet, wet pain...
GRAB my heart and pretend we live like the Beaver's parents.

Bells around my neck marking me with the bright sound of Santa or the New Year's elf or the last pack-horse dumb shit mule or god help civilization to discover the nerd of the squeaky bed.

C'MON...C'MON, KEEP THAT JUMBLE COMING AT ME, THAT'S WHAT I AM HERE FOR.

To be chained at the bed of the Emperor Princess, Tongue Mistress, that girl to love somebody with the power of frustration.
Give it up.
That magic sin that has my *NAME* written all over it.
Eating breakfast when the sun went down and I watched the moon and the star gods crying all over the sidewalk.

Arachnid female jerking under the covers and spraying secret words about the air, words about which I care, I truly care.

*Over my shoulder I feel that ominous man with the crooking hands and the stare of death and teeth and dust and his eyes are so terrifying and they are* RED...
like a broken heart's blood.

And then I cannot find my pretty shoes in the JUMBLE.
Naked feet and the road before me is so hazardous...

With sharp rocks and jagged glass, hot embers and deep holes filled with needle-like thorns.

Turn it up so that I can see her smile better as they lock my ankles together and the ghosts hover about me.

Wood splinters pierce my back and frightening howls fill the air dancing with ugly faces.

And the fire licks like a leviathan tongue filled with buckets of slippery spit, and my body bucks with pain intersecting with the pleasure of a nuclear endless orgasm.

All of this cannot compare to even one of her searing kisses.

So I will just dive in,
pointing my toes and cutting the flames with a "10."

The rabbits cheered for fast and frisky sex.

The cats rubbed their whiskers waiting to scream furballs in the night.

The dogs in the auditorium were stuck together like Doolittles "pushme-pullme."

The lights came on and that JUMBLE never ends sparkling reflection in a crocodilian's eye.

I try to run away from it all in the room with the least light,
the place of easy flight.

I am starving for the Dream of the Luscious JUMBLE.
I can raise it up out of the residue of an episode in real life.
The tears I capture in a bottle are the only reality.
The tears in a bottle,
my truth.

# THE SEVEN RAGES

Bizarre shift of spatial consequences and I look inward.
Molars grinding pak choi and the malassimilation of leaves coagulates.
Intestines knotting like twisted twine.
Cool and smooth before me stands the jade panther.

The rubric in bold engraving almost screams in my cells,
calling forth cancer, malaria, delirium, and the seven rages of Lust.
Jade panther poised like a statue preparing for animation.
Coiled muscles cocked as only her eyes move,
following prey, following my astral form in this dominion.

My mouth opens, spewing protons and neutrons like billiard balls.
My eyes flash fire, crackle lightning, see beyond universes,
beyond beyond, beyond the beyond,
and the jade panther is frozen like weathered concrete,
clawed paws digging into rotten dried mud, sludge of forgotten epochs.
Purple wind spirals like a dust devil, picking up multi-legged creatures, furbearing insects, three eyed rose bushes, octopus-armed snails, winged seashells inhabited by skinless, hairless kangaroo tripeds, and I close myself to the graphics of wind and color.

My hands reach out and my fingers close, touching something tangible. Something familiar.
Vision flows through the tips of my fingers like micro-video-cams and I can glimpse the truth.
The truth of the jade panther which stills burns in my mind and the truth of the seven rages of Lust.

*Lingering sight upon exposed flesh*

*desire coursing through unreality*
*Expectations surreal*
*Fantasy metamorphosizing*
*Synaptic neuristor quivering internally*
*Aortic palpitations*
*Mental nudity dispersed chaotically to infinite receptor sites.*

Lust
Jade
Green eyes
Sleek panther
Forbidden
Anguish

Evaginate emotion.
I look down at the floor, cold tiles, and see a pool of clear liquid.
Shimmering puddle.
My eyes hurt.
Pool of tears.
I have been crying for hours, days, and my eyelashes are shaped like the points of stars.

The reflection in the pool is scary.
A scary quiet staring set of jade eyes.
And the strength comes rushing into me, connecting tissue, molecular exploding of power,
and the seven rages of the Lust flee screaming into some hidden uncharted world.
The power feels like the first taste of Jell-O or the first kiss, or the dream of falling.
> I fall in the intoxication of the power.
> I fall in.

> I fall.
> I fall in the stages of Love.

# CRY SORROW

Sand.
And seashells.

Fisherwoman stands upon the rocks, facing the sea.
Silhouette in the rising glow of morning.

Air.
And salt.

The lonely one, gazing, in thought, at the sea.
Watching the fishing, watching the water.

Gulls cry sorrow and the waves pound.
He sits, arms around his knees, upon the ground.

Early daybreak, with no clouds.
On the beach, a solitary Great Blue Heron, standing proud.

Fisherwoman wears a straw hat.
Sun begins the heat, turns up the thermostat.
The lonely one stretches and stands.
The light and wind touch his bare chest.
He sighs, deeply.

He turns and walks away from morning light.
Fisherwoman has made a catch.
Great Blue Heron, fish in beak, flaps into the light.
Gulls cry sorrow, and the waves pound.

# HEY MISTER

Sleeping in a puddle of sweet tears.
I sometimes lose touch.
If you believe anything I say with my voice, too bad you cannot see inside my thoughts.
I am tormented every minute, every second, every breath of oxygen, every pulse of the blood from my wild heart.
Nothing is cool, nothing is real, nothing is worth opening my eyes...
only to fill them with the sweet water.

Hey Mister do you know the way to Heaven?
I sometimes lose touch.
It is Easter Sunday, roll away the boulder.
If you believe, do you know the way to Hell.
I am taking the train to Purgatory, a place of tears.

There is another world out there, and another and another.
There are seven dominions.
The home of water and fire and vapor and lightning and stripes and horns and the realms of the twenty-seven gods.

I sit in the corner and shake and wrap my arms about my knees.
Where is the sun?
Where is the full moon?
Where is the sensation of life.
The drug is the sadness, the paralyzing fear.

The sleep is the place of the real sanity, the dreams of my desires, my nightmares making me feel more than the waking.
Tell me, Mister, WHAT THE HELL IS THE MATTER WITH ME?

# THE MOVIE

Just sit and watch the movie I have become.
Follow me with mountains that shift and fall.
Crawl with me to the depths, farther than earthworms, deeper
than lantern fish.
Sleep with me to have knowledge of the ocean.

I have talked with angels.
I have stumbled into halls of demons.
I have gotten drunk with the rebellious, the dead, the forgotten,
the lost souls.
I have flew in the sky a few times.

Sprayed liquor at the darkened doorways of the harlots,
kissing the razor blades dykes, licking salt of the cattle's block.
I am running in the syrup and sweating with mud queens,
mosquitoes plugging my nostrils, green mongrels, dogs with
snot from anthrax fever killing and eating away at the guts.
I try to rid myself of her photo, locking it away inside a hidden
icebox, setting the microwave timer on infinity, she comes a
scratching at the corners like some poison ivy vines come to life
chasing me through the woods to Gramma's house.
I always end up on a pitcher's mound in a graveyard.

Just sit and follow this movie I have become.
Too bad I won't be around to see the final credits.

# Single Silver Kiss

Dark and surreal atmosphere on a Sunday night.
Bewitching nuances from scattered eyes across a lighted field.
I almost trembled when i caught a glance from those sparkling
blues...
suggestions of atmospheric glimmers wavered before me like
invisible love fairies sprinkling love dust upon my head.

I watched from a distance like an unarmed hunter.
I watched entranced and mesmerized by her intimate secret
heart.
I could not take my eyes from her.
She smiled like a glittering gem and laughed like a diminutive
waterfall rushing over flat rocks on a hidden forest stream.
And I was taken away like a willing prisoner ...
handcuffed inside, my heart locked to whatever mysteries she
embodied.
And I was swept like a floating feather, an orange autumn leaf,
pollen drifting on the breeze towards my destiny.

I made her music and art,
I gave her my heart.
I gave her a single silver kiss,
and a porcelain white dove...
green eggs inside of a tiny nest.

We touched eyes...
we touched hands and electricity coursed through my arm like
blue flames under my skin.
We touched eyes...
my hand touched her face and I shivered like a young colt first
trying to gallop.
I never wanted to kiss anyone else again  in all my life, just her
, just her.
we touched eyes and i thought of her leaving me behind and
almost died.

Driving late at night I saw flickers of light.
I felt her hand in mine.
And we touched eyes...
and i delivered kisses to her heart,
and a rose's fragrance to stir the flame within her.

She is a vision, a glimpse at the edge of the lake.
Mystery ensconced within nature.
I daydreamed of backyard bar-b-que's, hayrides on Halloween,
watching children opening presents, our eyes always meeting
and smiling inside like two souls knowing their future has
become their present.

I saw flickers of light when we touched eyes.
and i fell deeply into those sparkling blues...
my heart drawn to be next to you.

Dark and surreal atmosphere.
my love pouring like lava from the earth,
the stars overhead twinkling with bright smiles.
And we kiss.
And we kiss.
And invisible love fairies sprinkle love dust...
the dust of our past leads us into a new future.

# OVERLOAD

Sometimes the brain can overload.

There are days of chaotic nervous fire in your belly.

I have been known to swim in the pool of tears.

Haven't we all felt a little sorry for ourselves?

Haven't we all wanted to smile, relax contently, and recline in our lover's arms.

Haven't we all wanted sex that explodes like a nuclear reactor, a lightning storm, the booming of a volcano, rivers of lava in our mind as we kiss and touch and taste.


In this world of searching for those things I can tell you this,

We have to grab erotic excitement when we can.

We have to pull ourselves up over the edge of the cliff that drops off into a Wile E. Coyote canyon before we fall desperately to the bottom with a plop and a puff of dust as we hit rock bottom.

Depression is only a few hours away from happiness in any given person.

Sadness is only a heartbeat away from laughter.

Tears are universal, they are a reaction to both sides of the emotional spectrum.


Weird, huh?


Remember that nervous fire in your belly.

That's the fire of unknown origin.

The fire smolders when you take away the special ingredients.

The fire comes from trying too hard, trying to conform to a persona that belongs to a fictional comic book character.


Hey! But what about the other fire? The electric white hot sizzling fire.

The fire that travels in your veins.

The fire that feels great inside your heart, your hands, your mouth, behind your eyes.

This is the fire that I live for.
This is the fire that is love.
This is the consuming fire.
This is the fire that burns away depression, sadness, and quenches the soul.
This is the fire I long for.
The fire I desperately need.
The fire I want to feel inside me, again.
This is an addictive licking flame.
Burning that way, I can never be the same.


Light me up, baby.
Strike your match with those lips.
Put that hot flame against my skin.
Kiss me like a flamethrower.
Touch me with fingertips that glow with living candle wick flickers of heat.
Claw my back with the hottest rage of passion.
Scorch me inside and out, ride me into the lake of fire.
I look deep into your eyes and see flames of red flashing in the pupils.
Cook me in the bucking throes of a Wok.
Microwave my desire.
Make me fall in love with you.
Melt my heart.
Grind and feed my flames until I am only ashes in your hand, in your heart.
Oh, baby, I am smoking, my desire like a supernova, a global warming at the equator, a crematorium, oven baked pizza, crawfish boil pots, the aluminum foil on a TV dinner.
My desire bubbling over, boiling and sizzling on the stove of your skin.
I'm hot enough now.
Ready to eat.
Devour me and keep me from the bottom of the canyon for a few more hours.

Weird, huh?
Hey, sometimes the brain can overload.

# MR. PHONE

Run for cover.
Hide somewhere.
Assholes from hell are coming.

These guys call every night.
In the middle of your favorite show.
While you eat your supper on a TV tray.
"Need some aluminum siding, better long distance, a plot of dirt to be buried in?"

Please, Por Favor, No Mas, Quit dialing, touch toning me.
And then you call in to Mr. Voice Activated Computer.
The greatest stress relief is not Cardio Karate but Computer Man Kick Ass Session.
Line up the telecomputerresponse system guys and bust their butts.

I just want to reach my hand through that damn phone and grab wires and plugs and smash monitor screens, destroy hard drives and software, punch the holy shit out of that asshole voice saying, " for this push one for that push two for this for three and for that push for, if you do not have a touch tone phone you are fucked-asshole stay on the line for your next available customer service representative and meanwhile listen to Mozart rap or an infomercial or the self-help chat line...

Hold that thought.
There is no satisfaction from hanging up on a computer.
There is no relief of frustration for slamming the phone down while you exist only on hold, pacing the floor, tapping your fingers, thinking if only I could call once, just once, dammit and get a live human being on the line.
All I wanted to ask was just one little question, yes or no.
We don't want to punch a zillion buttons, to go from Mr.

Computer Voice to Mrs. Computer Voice to Uncle Computer Voice to Smart Ass Computer Voice to "please hold for the ...""STOP IT!"

I just made up my mind.
A stamp is thirty-two cents.
It is in the mail.

# RAINSTORM NOWHERE

I have never smoked a cigarette.
Nowhere.
I met you in a rainstorm.
Nowhere.
Crazy like a one blue-eyed horse.

Long blonde hair drags me to my knees.
In the air.
Your scent wiped like cologne on my cheeks.
In my tears.
Clouds move like orange brilliance and classical music.
I thought you were something else.
Nowhere.

Your mouth moved.
I couldn't recognize the bent syllables.
I often take trips to the Orient.
Nowhere.
Asian vacations, Bengal tigers and temples.
Nowhere.
The sky is purple just before it turns black.
Inside me.

Lost loves have ghostly voices.
Radio stations that whistle and static.
I bring to life with words from uncharted feelings.
Nowhere.
Go ahead and stand in the next rainstorm and remember me.
I had forgotten my umbrella.

# REALM

Into the realm of smoke and green tables
We trod like familiar emissaries
towards unfamiliar sustenance
and the awaiting game of colored orbs,
fighting sticks and trickery of the smirk.

My thoughts of my opponent
my adversary, my wench, my uncertain lover,
my mind watching through veiled eyes.
So sure her moves , her positions, her stance.
Lovely the way she absorbs me, revels in the maneuvering,
the winning flowing through her like wine from a Cossack's
flask.

And I watch all those hours.
And I want.
And I can see things in her.

This mystery deepens.
As I follow this new rainbow into shadows of another place.
A place of swirling music and bantered conversations.
A place where minuscule missiles fly.
A place of targets and talk.

I bravely speak thoughts of fire.
And in the blink of eyes and neon
she opens like a night blooming flower.
And we kiss.
Cascading into each other like two hidden fountains
in a secret forest.

We drink.
But moments.

We drink.
But sips.
Unquenchable kisses.

# SAVIOR

I can feel the burning of her touch,
her flesh so searing as it kisses mine.
I can cry and I could die and I could scream at the sky.
How could I be twisted in the rainbow's vise?
The many gods call to me to inhale the scents of the fiery lust.
A solitary beam of white-hot light shines deep into my iris,
oh my savior...
a woman is looking at me from across the bridge,
longing in her every movement.

I cannot move away,
pulled to the nails in my palms with my desires.

Dripping and slippery wet,
dew droplets hanging from my eyelashes as I look beneath me
at her face catching fire,
flicking her tongue at me, saliva covering her lips of red heat.
Arching my neck I suck in the atmosphere like a lost swimmer
regaining the surface.

I cannot move away, the biting of the nails in my ankles with the
connection of electric chemicals inside her soul.

I am charged.
I am excited down to the smallest molecule.
I am riding wave after wave.
I am ultra-conscious.
I am mega-alive.
I am electrons, neutrons, protons, spinning out of any
semblance of scientific sense.
I have stopped breathing.
I am the blackness of exploding spots behind closed eyelids.
We are shadows of each other.
Blinking stars of near-light flash in chaos around my face.

Savior, lover, obsession, redemption in her smile
I fly from the cliffs...

She is an animal of myself and we are joined in the pain, the fear, the DNA.
We have lived for centuries always together and apart.

I cannot move away.
I flex my fingers, feeling the pain, which reminds me I AM STILL OF THIS EARTH.

Don't make a sound.
There is an outside.
We cannot move away, OR DENY.

The nails and the blood...
The splinters of the cross in my bare back...
Her eyes...

# WE

This is the sound of your drifting color.
The color of your dreams.
Start to move your body from the inside out and follow the rhythm of your own heart.
I will touch you gently.

Scarlet splashes across our landscapes of sand and clover.
Fields of infinite flowers, exotic fragrances that saturate the senses.
I can feel you beginning to sway with the sound of the color.
I watch you intently.

Descend with me into the sound.
We hold onto one another like lost lovers on the edge of darkness.
Our eyes are closed but we see the same sight, the scenes of color.
The midnight blue envelopes us as we fly over chasms filled with blood.
Our finger tips merge and our hearts beat simultaneously.
The air rushes around our skin as we clasp each other in flight, face to face.

I whisper into your ear, "We are one, my love."
The sky welcomes our embrace.
The color shifts and we stand on top of the tallest pinnacle at the height of the world.
We open our eyes.
I stare at you like you are the last gulp of oxygen on the planet.
I can smell you and I hear the sound of color, the sound the wind makes when it caresses your sleek skin.
I am jealous of the wind's touch.
In the soft pink of dusk we stand at arms length and merge into each other with only our eyes and our hearts, the spirits

projecting from our souls kissing one another above our bodies.

I fall to my knees.
Your hands are in my hair.
I listen intently to your heart with my head to your stomach.
There are tears in my eyes.
The sound of your drifting color intoxicates and coalesces into my soul.
I become your drifting color.
I begin to fill you up.
The wind stops and the sky is moved by our connection and begins to weep.

The light rain tastes like salt.
We began to dance the dance of the water sprites.
The rain splatters down like love, immersing us, drenching, saturating, soaking, pouring down on our dance.
Wet feet splashing in the forming puddles, smiles on our faces, dancing on top of the tallest pinnacle at the height of the world.

We dance and embrace.
A lone white bird circles.
The sky clears and a rainbow slowly spreads its drifting sound of colors from one side of the world to the other.
The rainbow lowers until it merges color with the sound of our color.
We stand together beneath the merging of colors and are showered with a golden cascade of millions of bright cold sparks.
The sparks touch our skin like thousands of tiny kisses and are absorbed.
The sparks travel inside our bodies until we have become phosphorescent.
We have transcended.
Our hearts are glowing golden and growing, pulsing together.

The layers of humanity fall away.
There is no more need for skin, skeletal structure, or nervous system.
We are pure.
We have become our souls.
We have become pure love.
We have become.
We have.
We.

# Wolf

Doctor tell me, "Is Elvis God?  The second coming?"
Tell me, "Is the king really dead?  Or has he risen in Tasmania,
Jamaica, Borneo,
The Galapagos Islands, Fiji, Iceland, Vegas?"

Lying here on your couch I fell asleep with my eyes open as you
interpret
my dreams projected upon the big screen on the wall.
The world is better off being run by the perfect humans,
the bi-sexual women who experience all of the senses,
all of the living, all of all.

It is in the eyes, the clue to the wolf.

Doctor, "How I am bleeding away invisible sources of my
existence?"
Clothes make the man, bullshit!
Nudity makes the man.  Nudity of the mind.
The unstable are the genius's.

It is in the hunger, the feast of the wolf.

Lying here in the cramped chair I see you take notes upon clean
white sheets,
white sheets from hard bark of the rainforest trees.
Lying here as you study me, what makes me move, react, think,
desire, pay attention, to eat.
 They way I will eat her when I'm hungry.

The wolf lusts for the forest and the open snow.
The wolf longs to take her in his mouth.
Doctor you can only write what I say, what you hear, see.
Inside the werewolf ravishes your white skin, and you gasp,
ripping the white smock to become alive again.

Doctor, tell me, "Is the king really dead?
Are you clinging to me for the money or the pleasure?
Are you sure Elvis is dead?"

Tell me, please, am I insane or normal,
or does it really matter as long as I am not dangerous?

The wolf in our minds lies dormant waiting for his opportunity.

Centuries... always together and apart.
Doctor, don't be afraid.
The eating of her is the pleasure.

# Purr of the Panther

Reclining naked, my head in her hands, my thighs stretched across her sister's lap,
I need this poison.
I suck them up like a ravenous octopus, a flesh devouring lethal squid, and they both caress my chest, my neck, my stomach, all of my taut skin.

We barely talk.
We stare deeply through each other's skulls, into the other realms, that place of escape, sexual ecstasy, beyond the pleasure, beyond emotion, into the dominions, the domiciles of revelation, receptors, astral projection.
We feed off of each other like a squirming herd of seals, the fierce attack of a piranha school, like an eclipse of the sun.

I began to move slowly on her.
Her eyes never leave mine.
The sister touches my spine with fiery flicks of her tongue, raking gentle nails tracing each vertebrae like razor blade skis.

Purring sounds from deep within my throat as I shift and blend and flow...
alternate tasting of the sisters, drinking gulps of the flower petal fountains in the magic places, the spaces of soft honey, gooey, sticky, sweet, dripping juice, wet and strong and oozing just for the lapping of my panther's tongue.

I am the cat.
I am the night-visioned leopard.
I am the crouching, and the leaping, springing panther, mottled with the dark and the light, the shades of gray in the shadows of the flickering dozens of candle flames.
I growl and twist my body, wriggling and thrusting, scratching and biting, saliva spread like a delicious drug across tan skin.

I engorge myself upon their uninhibited passion.
I fulfill their wanton desires.
I become the only lover, the panther, every lover.
I revel in their pleasure, their cries for mercy, for soft words that I whisper as they beg and whimper in the throes of rolling oceans.
The sister's eyes are half-open-half closed.
Their legs are entwined like root systems.
I watch rivulets of sweat swim crooked courses across their amazon bodies.
They lie exhausted in a pool of saturation.
I am the proud panther sitting erect upon the tallest rock, licking his paws clean,
licking their taste from my skin.
I watch them look at me with little smiles of satisfaction on their faces.
I kiss them, softly, gently, locking eyes to remind myself that somewhere lies love.
I watch them leave.
I recline on the floor, breathing, after our journey.
I think about love.
I can still smell their sweetness on my skin, my face, my hands, and I start to cry.
I am the panther.
I hunt alone.
Searching for my mate.
I think about love.
I abandon myself in pleasure as distraction and sport, erotic excitement and bizarre obsession...
but I think about love.
I am the lone panther and I hunt.
I hunt for the love of the only one on the planet.
I purr softly...
I...think...about...love.

# Shadow Man

At the edge of the scary woods I stand,
Like slow water or rumbling clouds
And the depths whisper...
With haunting, invisible, mysterious terror.

The crackling of twigs and sticks snap, snap, snapping.
The wind afraid to disturb the eerie serenity
And my blood is thick and slow
Like that instant before the alpha adult calls your name.

I stand there intently peering into the impenetrable chaos of
vegetation.
I stand there about to involuntarily urinate.
I stand there like a piece of ice, slowly melting into a puddle of
trepidation.
And I here my name called from within the trees.

A calling as chilling as a broken igloo.
My eyes stare into infinity, open wide,
Wide and bulbous like a strangled screech owl.
Do I dare to step towards the ghostly calling, the cryptic woods,
the certain danger.
Do I dare?

One foot slowly slides backwards as my other slides forward,
Caught between fear and mortal terror, I stand in immobile
indecision.

When I was younger I played on a tin slide.
The height of the slide intimidated us all.
Until we conquered our fear.
We slid each day laughing and screaming,
Flying down the slide with adrenaline and excitement.
Once I fell off the top and ripped my shorts and ripped my
skin...

And poked my eye on a big screw.
Fear came back and my caution returned forever.


I stand near the twisted trees and hear my name,
 whispered like death.
A black shadow moves within the woods.
I almost turn to run.
I almost step forward one more time.
From somewhere far away I hear my dead grandmother calling
me home.
And I remember she had a Canada goose with a broken wing.
And I remember she saved me
from a large white turkey gobbler, with a broom.
I remember she was safety.


In my brain writhes a tangled bundle
of long sleek black snakes
Like octopus tentacles curling around each other and the
terrible hissing...
Hissing like the emptying of the pool float on a rainy Sunday.
I stare at the woods but I see the snakes and the poison and the
erect tails of scorpions.


Lightning strikes and in an instant I can see a shrouded form
standing in the woods,
Grotesquely beckoning me with a amorphous hand,
The shadow barely saying my name, my social security number,
my birth date,
Licking his lips like a slathering pit bull,
 chained too close to the house.


And then the thunder growls in the distance and I crouch,
ready to flee.
The moon dances slowly dodging the black clouds of the
approaching storm.
I feel the wind flex itself and a fat raindrop strikes my lips.
I taste the salt of blood in the drop.

I start walking towards the scary woods like a hypnotized zombie.

I feel alone.
I cry tears as I walk with heavy feet.
I shake and tremble as I feel myself pulled forward.
I try to look back at my house, my love, my life,
I try with eyes frozen like a cracking dried contact lens.
I am alone meeting the scary woods.

Stepping within the tangle of forest I cannot breathe.

As my heart still beats,
My mind calms.
The shadow-man reaches for me.
The trees bend down around me like a cage.
And the lightning strikes nearby in silence.
The sound of the storm is drowned by an overpowering cessation of sound.

And then I remember our song.
With a wicked cold hand touching my shoulder
And a chill enveloping my skin,
I shake my shoulders free.
I throw snakes and scorpions from my sky.
I embrace the vision of my true love
And hold her like courage.
And I sing our song.
And I listen to my own words.
And I heed them and dance.

Amidst death and fear...
Amidst mystery and uncertainty...
I find the strength to dance.
The hope of the dance sets me free.
The dance leaps in my heart and my soul.
And the trees fall back,

And the shadow flies away in another burst of lightning.
And my home is brightly lit.
My true love calls me home.

I am soaked from cool rain.
A cleansing water from the sky
Pours over my skin.
And my heart beats with renewed passion.
My love is fierce like the lightning.
Our dance fills me.
Afraid of the tin slide,
But in life and death, pleasure and pain,
I will always be dancing with my bride.

# Skin House

I will come for you.
You are special, so special to eat...
I will sex for you.
If you are formed...if you are driven...if you are saturated...if you
are...ready to escape into me, drink of me, capitulate with me.
What is your name?

I lie here upon the floor, sprawled, awaiting your mouth.
I am drunk with exotic pleasure.
You scream with expectations.
Baby, baby, baby, oh, la te da, la te do, play hop scotch with my
tongue.
To get you off, switch that place in your mind from just the sex
to the eclipse of climax.
What is your name?

If it escape that you want, I am where you want me to be.
If you need that, call me with whispers on your lips.
Taste my desire, the flames that burn on my fingertips like flesh
candles.
There is the time I came for you.
There is capitulation.
There is a new religion.
There is a skin house.
We go there and move around the floor without using our feet.
What is your name?

"Does it matter?"
Volcanoes vibrate the ground on distant islands, the molten
earth lying dormant for centuries until orgasm.
What is your name?
Como se llama?

It matters.

# The Dust Bunnies Parade

The bear sits in the corner, solitary and amusing.
Without claws, without teeth, without a will...
Quiet bear lurches left and watches the dust bunnies parade.

Dainty, tiny, rocking chair little miss Hiedi,
Tippy toes frolic,
 watching bear's woes.

Two days alone, fur bear frowns,
Ears bent down,
Shiny black obsidian eyes stare.

Twinkle feet, ringlet curls,
Chubby sweet girl,
Dancing like a lost ballerina,
On a banana.

Across the room, she glides and falls,
And cries and stops.
She sees the corner bear,
With his enduring black stare.
A twist of hair,
And she grabs the bear.

The bear sits in the windowsill, solitary and satiated,
Without claws, without teeth, still no will.
The dust bunnies parade.

# The Sinless Sea

Glancing at the depths of the deep I see a myriad of life.
A life denied me in this cascade of color.
I dream of swimming without effort.
 I roll like a sleek form in the cold waters off Alaska...
The warm tropical waters of the Caribbean,
The wet wonderland of Atlantis.

In my lover's arms I swim safely.
In my dreams I have slippery fins and hungry gills.
I am a torpedo of shocking speed underwater.
I have seen God.

In the sea there are no sins.
Amongst the coral formations there are no forbidden fruit.
Octopi and Cuttlefish, Rays and Eels, Nautilus and Conch
All dwell in a quiet library of liquid and kaleidoscopic lights.
Nowhere in the tunnels of the sea caverns are there laws
written.

I can see all that lives unseen.
I have stared into God's eye.
I have drunk of the saltwater.
I have eaten of crustaceans and shellfish.
I have breathed the bubbles of the great whales passing.
And I cannot cry underwater.

The myriad of life began in the sea.
Adam and Eve swam through the oceans that covered the
earth.
Water dominated all that is earth.
We all were born underwater.
Atlantis, the first city, spawned our ancestors.
There were no words, only bubbles and emotions.

We crawled out of the water and dried our slippery skins in the sun.
We lost our smooth flippers and tried to run.
We found air tickled our faces and earth tickled our feet.
We left the water and discovered a new heat.

I dream of the worlds of water.
The time before the land reared its lush head above the waves.
Our Father who art creator of life.
He who sprinkled the particles of life into the planet of water.
Our Lord, God, make us to swim down in the pastures under the sea.
Heaven in the waves.
We still dream of the water.

I am with my wife swimming in the water of the world.
Without sin, without poisoned air, without care.
I dream of the myriad life beneath the waves.
When all the land submerges once again,
I will leave the air and find Atlantis.
I will find Heaven under the sea.

Riding whales like ships,
I traverse the world of liquid.
Mystified by the colors of the giant squid,
I watch as infinite clusters of tentacles color the sea
Like fireworks in the forgotten sky.

God poured water on a sphere in the universe.
We are miniscule and should not wonder why.

# Wind War

The wind is furious and destructive.

It is annoying and devastating at times.

The wind is invisible thus enabling it...
a sanctuary from retaliation.

Infinite compulsion.
Freewill of overpowering omnipresence.
Unrestrained  irresistible imperceptible gusts of sheer will.

So I stand on the edge of the world,
And challenge the wind.

I stand there with weapons of honor,
Weapons of my own choosing to battle...
The unseen but felt enemy.

I pray to Supremity for victory.
I chant the rules of combat,
And sing my war song into the sky.

My right hand clenches the scythe,
My left grips the Stratosperic Implementic Extirpator.

I feel the wind's presence all about me,
Teasing me to rush into the fray without thought or strategy.
A forceful rush blasts into my form on the cliff.
I stumble and trip.
I fall to the stone surface, and rise again, unhurt.
I know the wind laughs at my clumsiness.
I grip the scythe and plant my feet, swinging mightily,
Slicing the invisible foe with the four-foot long steel blade.

I know the wind wounded as I hear a howl.

A counter gust propels me backwards and I fall,
Tumbling on the rocks and breaking my scythe.

I rise to one knee as the wind growls in my ears,
Gathering force to end my resistance,
And I strike with my other weapon.
One switch, two buttons, a ten second warming up period,
Laser adjustments, and a serious hum.

The war is over.
There is no more wind.

# I FEEL WATER

Narrowed eyes chasing me around that everclear cage,
that hypnotic haze that numbs even that tiny rage.

They wiggle and thrust that liquid tongue like a smooth python
coiling around justified lust, turning to dust.

I am just another number, a wild-eyed buckaroo, that can really
suck it up, back it up,
a long kiss like an ice-coated razor blade.

I feel the fade and take a nap in the big shade.

In the dream I see those yellow eyes staring like hungry cats,
and I cannot even breathe, the passion overcoming me... And
they pounce and rend and tear and the pain is lovely.
Fiery kisses like a blowtorch of desire,
and the Jester cries, "Hanging on the bull's tail, a purple scent
and a vapor trail..."

How does it feel to bite the one who makes you drip,
with a slippery whip?

I feel water,
at the edges of my eyes,
and it tastes like blood.

# CARDS

Deal 'em.
Life is a deck of cards, Roy Rogers.

I am the Jack of Hearts.
The Kings are all the married men.
The Aces are the millionaires that abound in the strip clubs.
And holy hell, the Queens are all the women, all of them.

The Queens of Clubs are the wild ones, never loyal, never settle.
Stay away, except for random nights of exotic frolic.
The Queens of Diamonds are the exquisite beauties, luscious like chocolate melting in your mouth but dangerous, poison for your soul, heartbreakers, life suckers, mind melters, loving no man ever as much as themselves.
The Spades Queens belong to all men, worship at the home, the keeper of children's dreams, and the nurturing mothers to the planet, from kittens to cows, from backyard B-B-Q's to fish fries, sleeping in the hay barn with husbands and washing possum blood from little boys.

And then there is the elusive, the almost invisible, nearly extinct, Queens of Hearts.
She is a gem in her soul mate's eyes, loyal for life, made only as one man's wife.
The search goes on.
Deal 'em.
Games of Poker.
Games of "Go Fish."
Crazy Eight, Blackjack, Uno, more games of Uno, which is safe and fun.
"Go Fish," "Got any Jack's," yes, I am one.
Games of Follow the Queen, Canasta, Gin Rummy, two whiskeys to dull the length of the search for the Queen of

Hearts.

Some people get seven cards, some five.
Some are born into full houses or flushes, hands full of aces, straights with Kings and Queens, Jacks, and the Ripper.

"21."
Deal 'em, God.
I'll raise you and I need four more cards.
I need a Queen of Hearts.

Ladies and Guys who drink beer out of cold bottles, I just need a Queen of Hearts to break even for the game.

I swear... I will never fold.

# EVOLUTION

Crossing over the waterways on flat fragile boats
I conceal myself in shrouded cloaks soaked with the musk of
civet cats.
I can see the torches of the enemy on the distant shores.

When I was young the children were sold to renegades.
I escaped to a different fate.
A life of fear and mystery,
Student of the science and the taste of true magic,
The scent of death and power.

I heard the clank and roll of the tanks crushing human bones.
I saw past the charade of real life.
I watched as many died to appease the gods.
I survived.

This world is gray and the yellow sun never penetrates to our
skin.
On an afternoon with drizzling rain I saw you.
Your hair was wet and your eyes haunted like a trapped rabbit.
I stared with fascination that you were even here.
One whisper on your lips and the day was new.

I followed you to secrets and evolution.
Your eyes shined in the cave like stars
And the tanks rolled overheard belching fire and disaster.
Hiding with you, moving from sanctuary to danger,
We hid on the boats of the waterways.

My choice of life changed with you.
The Seekers fight the war and the tanks roll on.
The Season of the Snake holds us tightly
And our home is only dirt and rubble.

The magic grows with the child.
The road takes us through the burning and the wire.
We hold hands and our skin is the clue that we live.

In another hour the planes will be high in the sky.
The refugees will die.
The shadows are what we have become.
Seekers stride forth, their red eyes probing for resistance.

It is snowing now.
The life we carry is the hope.
The wind blows through your hair
And we follow the path through empty buildings.

There is a leviathan fire in the distance.
Our hope kicks inside the mother.
Religion caused humanities downfall.
We wander to stay alive.
The Hindus fight the Christians,
The Jews fight the Buddhists, the Moslems hate them all.
And it is snowing.
The planes burn streaks in the gray sky.
The urn is hidden in a secret grotto.
The science, the evidence, the magic
Is the truth.
Our hope cries out in a new gray world.
And the snow has stopped.

# THE FUTURE OF THE SEA

Waves crashing on the rocks of a tattered shoreline,
And I am as still as a weathered beaten tree.
I see the hundreds of creatures moving in herds,
Wildebeests of the tundra, yaks of the high mountains
 zebra of the desert, and the many following predators.

All of life moves to the sea.

There is a candy wrapper blowing along the beach.
M & M's.
Sea lions bark incessantly.
I miss humans.

I am naked.
I am not cold.
I am the only and the one.

A polar bear strides by ignoring my stance.
A group of Oryx walk along the beach
moving into the sand dunes behind the rocks
searching for tender grasses.
The salt air stings my eyes.

Creatures keep coming in larger numbers to the sea.
Hyenas cackle like crazy grackles.
The elephants are so few and they walk like prehistoric gods in
the sand.
I used to have a gun.
It is useless without bullets.

I eat berries and melons.
The world is my paradise.
The sea is calling all the beasts forward.
The tide is the source.
The tide is Neptune's song.

I can only watch as the tide rises.
I know someday soon their will be only a craggy snow capped peak above the sea.
I know that soon it too will disappear.
Standing on the rocks above the ocean I see a humpback whale surface.
I can see its eye.
I know the future.

# The Eagle Omen

I swear it is true.
A lie is a whisper of truth.
The eagle flies like an omen.

I saw a man in black
Standing high on the cliff above the lake.
I used to watch the sunset
Until I saw his eyes.

I had a mouse in my pocket
To save him from being killed by a school bus.
A wicked boy stepped on him anyway.
The sunset seemed far away.

I think about the days of my youth.
There is not a way to go back.

Pastures of lion grass and solitary pecan trees
Are like an oasis to me.
The lake is still out there
But I haven't been back.

I think about the days of my youth
And of how I miss the hours in the fields.
At night bullbats zoom like jet fighters
And I remember the first time I heard the truth.
I was in Canada and she was by my side.
An eagle flew across the sky like an omen.

It is true.

# ABOUT THE AUTHOR

Doug Hiser is an author of several books and a professional fine artist of all media, illustration, sculpture, and collage. After winning the Houston Poetry Slam in 1993 he published three poetry chapbooks, SHARDS OF LIES, THE SEVEN RAGES, and WHISKEY MOON. He grew up in Santa Fe, Texas and graduated from the University of Houston CL as Student of the Year in 1996. His art adorns galleries and has won numerous awards. He is currently working on two new novels. He lives in Dickinson, Texas with his wife, Gayln, and their many birds. He enjoyed an instant of fame while appearing on the television show AMERICAN GLADIATORS in 1992. Doug and his wife are avid soccer players and love all sports.

# ABOUT GREATUNPUBLISHED.COM

www.greatunpublished.com is a website that exists to serve writers and readers, and to remove some of the commercial barriers between them. When you purchase a GreatUNpublished title, whether you order it in electronic form or in a paperback volume,  the author is receiving a majority of the post-production revenue.

A GreatUNpublished book is never out of stock, and always available, because each book is printed on-demand, as it is ordered.

A portion of the site's share of profits is channeled into literacy programs.

So by purchasing this title from GreatUNpublished, you are helping to revolutionize the publishing industry for the benefit of writers and readers.

And for this we thank you.

www.ingramcontent.com/pod-product-compliance
Lightning Source LLC
Chambersburg PA
CBHW071405170526
45165CB00001B/188